AS Religious Studies

REVISION GUIDE

AS Level Religious Studies
Components 01, 02 & 03

OCR (H173, H573)

Matthew Livermore

AS Religious Studies OCR (H173) REVISION GUIDE

From a Christian perspective

© 2016 Matthew Livermore

AS Religious Studies OCR specifications and past exam questions © OCR. References are included from the Oxford English Dictionary, some meanings are omitted, changed slightly or added to. Bible quotes refer to the New International Version.

ISBN: 978-1-78484-156-0 (pbk)

ISBN: 978-1-78484-157-7 (hbk)

ISBN: 978-1-78484-158-4 (ebk)

ISBN: 978-1-78484-159-1 (kin)

Published in the United Kingdom by PushMe Press.

www.pushmepress.com

Introduction

The new OCR RS A Level has been designed to be fuller and more rigorous, linking more coherently to a study of Theology or Religious Studies at university. Whilst retaining much of what was essential to the old "Philosophy and Ethics" RS A Level, it has broadened to include a study of some of the essential debates in philosophical theology: This has the effect of rounding-out some of the topics from the philosophy and ethics sections. Thus the "Christian Thought" module includes a study of Augustine on Original Sin, a section on natural and revealed theology, as well as modern debates in Feminist Theology and a study of the work Dietrich Bonhoeffer. This should provide a richer range of thought and thinkers from which to draw on in the philosophy and ethics modules. For instance, the study of Augustine should deepen student understanding of the problem of evil in the philosophy module, or the free will and determinism debate in the ethics module. The A Level will cater for a broad range of students wishing to take a further study of either philosophy or theology at university, whilst giving a stronger sense of the type of challenge involved in undergraduate studies.

Assessment has changed mainly in the weighting of AO1 and AO2 (assessment objectives - 1 being knowledge and understanding, 2 being analysis and evaluation). There is now greater emphasis on AO2, and there is also an increase in the marks allocated for answers.

Students are often surprised when they take A Level Religious Studies at just how different from GCSE it is, not just in the level of challenge, but in the subject matter as well. This can be a pleasant or an unpleasant surprise, depending on whether you wanted more of the learning-religious-views-on-abortion type of lesson, or not.

Good luck with your studying.

How to use this book

The OCR Religious Studies AS offers a wide range of choice for the teacher and student to pick from. There are **THREE** one hour and fifteen minute exams: one Philosophy, one Ethics and one from a perspective of religious thought.

This book provides you with detailed summaries of all parts of the OCR AS Religious Studies Components 01 (Philosophy of Religion), 02 (Religion and Ethics) and 03 (Developments in Christian Thought).

We have put extra resources on our website which you can access by scanning the code at the end of the chapter with your smartphone. The website resources are also organised under the specification headings. The code will take you directly to the module you have scanned and you can browse between modules on the site. You will find Key Quotes, Practice Questions and more. If you are reading a Kindle version of this book, you can click on the link at the end of each chapter.

At the beginning of each chapter, you will find a list of key words and their definitions. Many of these key words are in **BOLD** in the text so that you can see them used in context. In places, other words are highlighted as prompts for you to remember the content.

Contents

Philosophy of Religion

Religion and Ethics

Developments in Christian Thought

Philosophy of Religion

(H173/Component 01)

Philosophical Language and Thought

The Existence of God

God and the World

Introducing Philosophy of Religion

In this module much of the foundation for the whole A Level is laid. The study of ancient philosophical influences in Plato and Aristotle's thought is properly basic to any understanding of religious philosophy, ethics and Christian thought. This is because these two philosophers have bequeathed an epistemology (theory of knowledge) and an ontology (study of existence/being) that has been profoundly influential on the development of Christian culture. In other words, Plato's theory of knowledge has moulded strands of thought within western culture that are still influential today in such spheres as education and aesthetics. Equally, Aristotle could be said to have been influential on everything from medicine to law.

The topics in the philosophy module reflect this:

- The idea of soul as opposed to body

- The classical arguments for God

- Religious experience

- The problem of evil

all reveal fundamental debates about the way we attain knowledge:

- What should be kept in or left out of a study of "reality"

- The nature of the human condition

- Whether faith can ever be a prerequisite for certain types of knowledge

- Whether there are rational or evidential arguments which can lead to knowledge of God

- Whether matter is all there is, or if 'matter' is other than what is currently understood by science

Simplistic religious notions of "soul" are challenged - what is this thing called soul and how is it supposed to interact with body?

But materialism is not let off the hook either - how can it give a coherent account of itself and avoid challenges that point out that it is based on a paradox? For instance if we are meant to believe in materialism, presumably that is because it is rationally worthy of belief - but given that for a materialist the "mind" is simply a "bunch of tricks" as Daniel Dennett calls it, questions arise about what it can possibly mean for such a phenomenon to rationally hold a belief.

THE FORMS

Plato

Plato (428-348 BC) was a philosopher in ancient Greece, whose teacher was Socrates and whose pupil was Aristotle. He has had a profound influence on the development of Western Thought, so much so that A N Whitehead, in his "Process and Reality", has said that:

> *"The safest general characterization of the European philosophical tradition is that it consists of a series of footnotes to Plato."*

The focus here is on Plato's **THEORY OF KNOWLEDGE**, which is a branch of philosophy called **EPISTEMOLOGY**. Such questions as what constitutes knowledge, belief and opinion, how we are justified in holding something to be true, and the relationship between morality and knowledge are at the heart of this chapter.

KEYWORDS

- **FORMS** - The essence or idea of something which is universal and non-spatial, and which is prior to a particular thing, eg. The Form of Triangle is the true triangle, of which all actual triangles drawn on paper or anywhere else are mere copies

- **FORM OF BEAUTY** - The essence or idea of beauty, not itself a beautiful thing

- **PARTICULAR** - An individual object, which has existence in relation to its Form

- **KNOWLEDGE** - Justified true belief

- **OPINION** - Knowledge of particulars, a mixture of truth and falsity

- **EPISTEME** - Greek for knowledge

- **DOXA** - Greek for opinion

- **ANALOGY OF THE CAVE** - Plato's story to illustrate the difference between the World of Forms and world of particulars

- **INTELLIGIBLE** - Capable of direct intuition without need for discursive reason - knowable through the intellect

- **SENSIBLE** - Capable of being experienced through the senses

- **RATIONALISM** - Belief in supremacy of reason and a priori knowledge over empirical methods of knowing

- **EMPIRICISM** - Belief that all knowledge is based on experience acquired through the senses

PLATO'S UNDERSTANDING OF REALITY

Plato's reliance on reason rather than the senses

Plato's understanding of reality is formed by his interpretation of pre-Socratic debates about the nature of the world. In particular he sets out to answer questions about the possibility of knowledge when everything is changing, and therefore has no permanent essential self. He also tries to answer questions related to **THE ONE AND THE MANY** - ie. if there was only really one thing, or if there were many things. To us these seem odd questions, but they form the basis of a theory of knowledge which is still influential today.

Plato's quest

How can we have knowledge of changing things?

HERACLITUS (a pre-Socratic philosopher) said **PANTA RHEA** - everything flows - in other words there is no abiding essence to anything. Plato was working in the shadow of this problem.

Why was it a problem? Because if I know something is a certain way, but that thing changes, I can no longer be said to have knowledge of that thing. Even more basic than this is that if everything is changing, then nothing has an essence - the very notion of essence relies on the fact that there is an unchanging core of something - and if nothing has an essence then nothing is really knowable.

Take as an example the difference between knowing that the interior angles of a triangle add up to 180 degrees, and knowing that Burford Brown chicken eggs have slightly more orange yolks than other eggs. My certainty about the first proposition is far greater - indeed it is as great as it is likely to ever be - and not because everyone says that the interior angles of a triangle add up to 180 degrees. It is because if I investigate I will be able to see that from the very nature of angles and triangles, it is impossible that it could not be true. Whereas, although my experience tells me that all the Burford Brown eggs I've seen in the past have had more orange yolks, that may not be the case for all Burford Brown eggs, or ones I may see in future.

MATHEMATICAL KNOWLEDGE is really analogous to the kind of knowledge that Plato requires in order to truly know anything. Plato argues that even though everything is changing, and that most of the time when we think we know something, we really don't - we have an opinion which is not the same thing. There is still the possibility of **TRUE KNOWLEDGE**. If there wasn't, it wouldn't even be possible to have an opinion about something, because to have an opinion is to be right in some ways and wrong in others. In other words, opinion only makes sense against a background of knowledge about what is actually the case.

What are these elements of true knowledge, which are not mere opinion, and are completely certain? They are called by Plato **THE FORMS**.

Plato's argument for what he calls the **FORMS** can be summarised in the following way:

- **PARTICULAR** - All things experienced through the senses are particular things

- **WE NEVER SENSE ABSTRACTS** - We can sense a beautiful rose but not beauty itself

- **BEAUTY** - Many things can be beautiful, so beauty is a property they share, so there must be something called beauty which can be shared by different things, even though not accessible through senses

- **FORM** - This universal idea of beauty is an example of what Plato called a Form

- **FORM OF BEAUTY** - For Plato, the form of beauty manifests itself in different particulars, eg. a rose, a face, or a sunset

- **DISTINCT** - But why should there be something called "the Form of Beauty" which is separate from particular beautiful things?

- **INDESTRUCTIBLE** - Because if you destroyed all beautiful things you would not destroy "beauty"

- **INDEPENDENT** - So particular beautiful things participate in the form of Beauty, but it is independent of them

THE NATURE OF KNOWLEDGE IN SUPPORTING THE THEORY OF FORMS

Analysis of knowledge gives more support to Plato's separation of particulars from Forms. **PARTICULARS** are always a mixture of properties. Therefore, a ball will partake of the form of roundness, shininess, blue-ness etc.

Particulars are also only relative to what they are. For example, something may be big, shiny or round but only relative to other (perhaps) bigger, shinier and rounder things. This means that our knowledge of any particular thing will always be **BOTH X** and **NOT-X**. In other words it will both be shiny and yet not shiny when compared with something shinier.

However, if particulars are only relatively shiny, large or round, then we cannot have true knowledge of particulars. Why? Because knowledge can only be of what is, never of what is not - you cannot know what is not true.

If something both is x and is not-x we cannot have knowledge of it

There is nothing beautiful that does not sometimes seem ugly, or seem ugly to some, or is only beautiful for a short time, but that means that it is, in some sense, both beautiful and not-beautiful.

But as we said before, you cannot have knowledge of what is not, so there must be another faculty at work when people disagree about the beautiful thing. Of course, that is opinion;

Plato argues knowledge and opinion (or **EPISTEME** and **DOXA**) are two different faculties.

Why? Because opinion can be mistaken but knowledge cannot: **YOU CANNOT KNOW WHAT IS FALSE**.

And as knowledge is about what is real, but ignorance is about what is not real, ie. does not exist (because if you are ignorant about something you know nothing of it at all), but knowledge of particulars seems to be somewhere in the middle of these two states (both x and not-x) then there should be a faculty somewhere in the middle.

This faculty is **OPINION**: It is not knowledge because it can be mistaken (see above), but it is not ignorance either, because you cannot have an opinion about nothing, opinion is always about something. Therefore, Plato argues that knowledge relates to the world of Forms and opinion relates to the world of senses. This means that the Forms must exist separately from the particulars.

THE NATURE & HIERARCHY OF THE FORMS

The Forms have certain fundamental properties:

- **SIMPLICITY** - The Forms are "one" - they only have the one property - eg the Form of Beauty is only beautiful. If they did not have this unity the forms would become particulars because they would become mixtures of properties

- **PERMANENCE** - Forms are unchanging. If they could change then that means they have become what they are or will become something else, which is clearly impossible as they either would not previously have been beautiful, or are not beautiful yet, which is a contradiction

- **PERFECTION** - Forms are the perfect examples - they are the standard by which the particular things which contain them are judged - if they were less than perfect they would not be the Form

- **SEPARATENESS FROM PARTICULARS** - Because of all of the above, Forms do not exist in time and space, and neither do they need to be manifested in particulars - they are the essence of themselves, in contrast to particulars which participate in these essences, but are not them

- **LOGICAL PRIORITY** - The Forms are what they are in virtue of themselves, whereas the particulars are what they are in virtue of the forms. Therefore, the Forms are logically prior to the particulars – the particulars are dependent on the Forms, which means there is a hierarchy, with the Forms at the top and the particulars further down

- **THE GOOD AS THE SUPREME FORM** - Just as the Forms are logically prior to the particulars, so the **FORM OF THE GOOD** is logically prior to the other Forms, because it is by this Form that all the other Forms are capable of being known; thus, the Form of Good is the Form of Forms. This is because the Forms of Beauty, Justice, Truth etc. are all themselves good, so they must in some sense participate in the Form of the Good, and the Good is at the basis of being able to know the Forms of Beauty or Justice or Truth

THE ANALOGY OF THE CAVE

The **ANALOGY OF THE CAVE** shows the journey that the philosopher makes from illusion to reality - from ignorance to the world of Forms.

A prisoner is chained alongside others facing a wall. Behind them is a fire and in front of that a raised wall, upon which objects are placed so that they cast their shadows onto the wall in front of the prisoners. One of the prisoners is freed, and first sees the fire, the objects and then begins the difficult ascent out of the cave. When he gets outside and his eyes become accustomed to the light he sees reflections of the moon and stars in water, then he sees them in the sky. Finally he sees the sun. When he returns to free the prisoners from the cave and tell them of the outside world they think he is mad and drive him away.

Each stage of the analogy has a meaning. They are:

- **THE CAVE** - The world of the senses

- **THE SHADOWS ON THE WALL** - Illusions: What we see and mistake for reality

- **THE CHAINS** - Ignorance

- **THE FIRE** - The sun

- **THE OBJECTS ON THE WALL** - Physical things

- **THE DIFFICULT ASCENT** - The dialectic – the process of arriving at truth

- **THE REFLECTIONS** - The process of understanding

- **THE MOON & STARS** - The Forms of justice, beauty etc.

- **THE SUN** - The Form of the Good

The purpose of the analogy and its relation to the theory of Forms

For **SOCRATES**, the teacher of Plato, education is not giving knowledge to those who lack it. That would be analogous to putting sight into blind eyes. It is rather turning the whole body and therefore the eye towards the light.

> *"But then, if I am right, certain professors of education must be wrong when they say that they can put a knowledge into the soul which was not there before, like sight into blind eyes.*
>
> *They undoubtedly say this, he replied.*
>
> *Whereas our argument shows that the power and capacity of learning exists in the soul already; and that just as the eye was unable to turn from darkness to light without the whole body, so too the instrument of knowledge can only by the movement of the whole soul be turned from the world of becoming into that of being, and learn by degrees to endure the sight of being and of the brightest and best of being, or in other words, of the good."*

Plato, The Republic, Book VII

The analogy illustrates important elements of Plato's theory:

▶ Knowledge is remembering

The effort needs to come from the individual to turn towards what is and away from what is not.

▶ The whole soul should be turned to the light

Education is not an intellectual exercise but a moral and spiritual conversion. This can be seen in the fact that the sun in the analogy reveals what exists by its light, just as we only know truly by the Form of the Good, all knowledge then has a moral dimension.

▶ The intelligible world and the sensible world are related

The latter is a shadow of the former. Just as the fire in the cave represents the sun in our physical world, so the sun in the analogy represents the Good, that by which everything which is, is made visible. Equally, we should take this as a prompt: Our sun, that by which we see, can only show us visible objects. We realise from the analogy that if our knowledge only extends to what we can see then we are stuck in the cave looking at the objects by the light of the fire.

This shows Plato's insistence that **RATIONALISM** is superior to **EMPIRICISM**.

EVALUATION OF PLATO'S THEORY OF FORMS AND CAVE ANALOGY

Do we need a separate "World of Forms" to explain how we can know anything?

Plato's theory in summary:

▸ **A theory of two worlds**

This is known as dualism.

▸ **Forms are one over many**

Whenever at least two things have something in common, the property they share in common is a Form.

▸ **Forms are paradigms**

Patterns or models on which things are dependent.

▸ **Things or particulars participate**

"There are certain forms, whose names these other things have through getting a share of them - as, for instance, they come to be like by getting a share of likeness, large by getting a share of largeness, and just and beautiful by getting a share of justice and beauty."

Phaedo, 130e-131a

Which means they are knowable on this basis:

▪ **GRASPED BY INTELLECT** - Knowledge of a particular, such as a vase, is not true knowledge, because the true vase is not known through the senses but rather grasped with the intellect

▪ **THE WORLD OF FORMS** - Contains all the non-spatial Forms which are behind the particulars - these Forms are distinguishable from the particulars in the same way that being is distinguished from becoming. The Forms actually exist, whereas the particulars only partially exist.

- **THE IDEAL STANDARD** - Without Forms as an ideal standard we would have nothing to appeal to when we make judgements - we implicitly assume the existence of the Form of Justice whenever we say that some particular thing is unjust, or more or less just than another thing.

Plato moves from some fairly innocuous initial observations to some rather drastic conclusions. Most philosophers agree that many of Plato's arguments for Forms are flawed and cannot offer support to his theory. However, it is often difficult to say exactly where the arguments are lacking, and students sometimes resort to saying "Plato has no evidence for his theory", which is partly understandable, but which on its own is just not adequate as criticism. Below I have tried to set out some of the major problems with the theory.

Evaluation

- **ONE OVER MANY IS NOT AN ARGUMENT** - "One Over Many" is not strictly an argument for the Forms. All it proves is that there are properties of things. Those properties might be **IMMANENT** - in this world, or they might simply be names we give to things - this is known as **NOMINALISM**.

- **THE THIRD MAN ARGUMENT** - Aristotle showed that the theory of Forms was subject to a criticism which reduced it to absurdity. If we have a collection of large things and their form "largeness" then we should consider the collection of things large, as well as the form "largeness" itself large. But in that case do we not have to appeal to a further form in order to consider largeness large? And why should we stop there?

This criticism undermines the idea that the Forms can be ideal standards, by showing that we would need to appeal to an infinite amount of Forms simply to make one judgement.

- **LACK OF EMPIRICAL SUPPORT** - It is not really surprising that Plato provides little empirical evidence for his theory, as he shows, especially in the analogy of the Cave, that he believes empirical data is next to useless in gaining real knowledge. Plato is a rationalist, and as such makes use of logic and A PRIORI reasoning for his proofs.

- **PRACTICAL EFFECTIVENESS OF SCIENCE** - However, from a modern standpoint, it looks suspicious that the theory has so little grounding in empirical data, and indeed, appears completely counter-intuitive. For instance, if this world is not really real, and the World of Forms is invisible and only knowable through the intellect, how is it that we are able to predict the behaviour of this world so well through scientific theories? And not just predict but also manipulate and make the natural world work for us through the use of technology? If it is all an illusion, should it be capable of producing such practical beneficial outcomes for us as medicine etc.?

- **GUESSING GAMES** - It is worth bearing in mind that Plato was not able to see the astounding success of science which would come nearly 1800 years after his death, but it is possible that even if he could have foreseen it he might still have pointed to the prisoners making guesses about the objects that threw their shadows on the wall in his Cave analogy and implied that science is still just a really sophisticated version of this game. For Plato, truth was never decided on the principle of practical effectiveness which many point to to assert the importance of science.

NEED MORE HELP ON PLATO?

Use your phone to scan this QR code

Aristotle

Aristotle (384-322BC) was a Greek philosopher who, alongside Plato has had a profound effect on western thought. His works have been influential in Law, Medicine, Botany, Theology, Physics, Ethics and many other areas. Thomas Aquinas was so indebted to him that he called him simply "The Philosopher". In this chapter we will see how his ideas about cause, and what makes something what it is have led to theories about the universe, human beings, and their purpose.

KEYWORDS

- **AITION** - Greek word translatable as "because" - cause or reason for something

- **CAUSE** - Explanatory principle for something's existence

- **EXPLANATION** - Reason or reasons given for why something is as it is

- **POTENTIALITY** - Possibility of being something

- **ACTUALITY** - The state of something's being what it is meant to be

- **ACTUALISATION** - Process by which a thing becomes what it is meant to be

- **POTENCY** - The ability something has to become something

- **ACT** - Something's existence as opposed to its potency

- **AGENT** - Actor, thing which is the cause of something else

- **EFFICIENT CAUSE** - The "how" of something

- **MATERIAL CAUSE** - The "what" of something - the matter it is made from

- **FORMAL CAUSE** - The characteristics or blueprint of something

- **FINAL CAUSE** - The "why" of something - what it is for

- **TELEOLOGY** - Explanation of something in relation to ends or goals

- **LATENT** - Unrevealed, lying hidden in something

- **PRIME MOVER** - Unchanging first cause or principle behind the change we see in everything

- **A PRIORI** - Relating to knowledge which proceeds from theoretical reasoning rather than empirical data

ARISTOTLE'S VIEWS IN RELATION TO HIS UNDERSTANDING OF REALITY

ARISTOTLE considered at the beginning of his Physics that we can only know something inasmuch as we can explain it,

> *"Knowledge is the object of our inquiry, and men do not think they know a thing till they have grasped the 'why' of it"*

For Aristotle, the word he used for the "why" of something was **AITION**, which has been translated as **CAUSE**, although **EXPLANATION** could also be used.

Aristotle draws a distinction between **POTENTIALITY** and **ACTUALITY**. He applies this to the process of change (or motion). Change is simply the process by which an object acquires a new form (very different from Plato's idea of form). The object has the **POTENTIALITY** to become something different, and change is the **ACTUALISATION** of the potential of one form of matter to become another form of matter. For example, the block of marble has the potential to become an actual statue. The statue is **LATENT** within the block of marble - the block of marble has the capacity to become a statue.

There are two important things to note:

- **POTENCY** and **ACT** are distinct; the marble cannot be both a block and the statue at the same time. In another example a piece of wood cannot be both potentially on fire and actually on fire at the same time therefore, change is this movement between potential and actual.

- As the object cannot be both simultaneously potential and actual, how does it move from one to the other? Aristotle says it needs an **AGENT** to move it, which he called the **EFFICIENT CAUSE**. This must in itself be in a state of actuality, not potentiality, ie. it must exist to be a cause of the change in the object.

  For example, you need actual water to effect the change of an acorn into an oak tree.

THE FOUR CAUSES

So because of these two principles - firstly that of the distinction between potency and act, and secondly that there need to be actual things to move potential things, Aristotle is able to derive his theory of the four causes. We can see how from this Aristotle got the first two of his causes:

- **FIRST CAUSE (MATERIAL)** - There must be matter which undergoes the change from one form to another, so in one sense, if we say "what is it?" of something or ask for an explanation of it we can say what it is made of. For example, the statue is made of marble: This would be then the material cause.

- **SECOND CAUSE (EFFICIENT)** - There must also be other actual things which are able to act upon that material and move it from potential to actual itself. These are the efficient causes. In the case of the block of marble it would be the sculptor with his chisel.

But Aristotle did not believe we could stop with just the material and efficient causes, the what and the how, as you might say. He believed that as the material has undergone a change of form in going from a potential thing to an actual thing, that part of its explanation was what the characteristics of it were. If we were to say to a person "what makes you the person you are?" they would normally not give a straight list of the elements that compose them such as carbon - they would probably talk about their upbringing or give a character trait, such as "I'm happy-go-lucky". Therefore we need to add another cause other than the purely material to get at a full explanation of a thing - we need to talk about its characteristics. For example, a chair is more than just some wood, it is an object with four legs and a space to sit.

- **THIRD CAUSE (FORMAL)** - In the statue example the formal cause would be its particular qualities of marble sculpted into the form of a body, head etc. The formal cause of something is the FORM of the thing - the pattern which makes it what it is - in the case of a building it would be the blueprint. This is not as easily understandable as the other causes, and has been seen as slightly controversial. Clearly, though, much debate surrounds the notion of a form and many agree that Aristotle's notion is no less flawed than Plato's.

- **FOURTH CAUSE (FINAL)** - This comes from the end of a thing, what it is for. This idea of a purposive cause is given by Aristotle because something's aim or goal is also an important part of an explanation of the thing. Aristotle gives the example of the final cause of walking, medicine, purging, surgical instruments etc. as all being for health. In the example of the statue, the final cause of the statue is for decoration or to give aesthetic pleasure. For Aristotle the aim of something can be seen as its greatest good, this is brought out in our use of language when we ask of an object "what is it good for?"

Aristotle's use of teleology

This emphasis on the telos, or the goal of something is a key part of Aristotle's thought. We remember that for Aristotle change is the actualisation of something's potential, with respect to its potentiality. In other words, something can only become what it has it in it to be - so a lump of wood can become a bed, or a block of marble a statue, but a piece of iron cannot become a wombat, nor can a human become a bird. The potential of something may be latent until something else acts upon it, but if that thing acts upon it in a directed manner and brings about its potential, then we can speak of the telos of something being achieved.

Modern science focuses on the efficient cause, when explaining the physical world, and in fact, the final cause is not considered. Of course, when we are talking of the human world, it makes sense to talk about why something happened in terms of a final cause. Some examples:

> *Why did John stay in last night rather than go to Mary's party? He wanted to avoid seeing Jane whom he dislikes.*

> *Why did you make that cake for Peter? I wanted to cheer him up.*

These are teleological reasons; They make sense in terms of what goal someone had in mind, and as such we would not get a very good understanding of those actions if we left them out.

THE PRIME MOVER

The **PRIME MOVER** is the logical outcome of the theory of four causes. If everything is moving from a state of potentiality to actuality, but everything potential requires something else actual to move it, then unless you posit some kind of unmoved mover, then you do not have a sufficient explanation for the movement of the whole series of things, or so Aristotle argues, because you cannot keep going back forever in a series of moved things, or you would never have a reason for the movement you currently observe.

You might notice that the argument for the Prime Mover is essentially the same as the **COSMOLOGICAL ARGUMENT** for God, which you will look at in the next module. The Prime Mover is an absolute, and has many similar characteristics to the Christian notion of God, but the two are not the same. In the same way that Plato's Form of the Good, is not really the same as God, even though it seems to fulfill a similar function, the same applies to the Prime Mover.

Another way of looking at the Prime Mover is from the standpoint of **FINAL CAUSE**. If everything has a reason or goal for its existence, then it could be said that the Prime Mover is the **ULTIMATE GOAL** of the whole collection of things called the **UNIVERSE**.

In summary then:

- **LOGICAL RESULT** - The Prime Mover is a logical result of the application of final cause to the whole universe

- **PURE ACTUALITY** - It attracts all to itself as the end or goal of all - there is no potentiality in it at all. It is pure actuality

- **CHANGE HAPPENS** - Remember the movement from potentiality to actuality is going on in all things – that is another way of saying that change is happening to them

- **SOME THINGS DON'T CHANGE** - Most things are changing (being generated and being destroyed) but some things are not changing in that way. Aristotle thinks here of the heavenly spheres, containing the planets and fixed stars, and which were considered to be nested around each other about the earth

- **CYCLICAL MOTION** - These are only undergoing change in the sense of cyclical motion, and are not (according to Aristotle) being generated or destroyed

- **MOVEMENT IS REALITY** - This is because their movement is the reality behind time itself, and for Aristotle time cannot be destructible. It is uniform and everlasting

- **MOVEMENT OF THE SPHERES** - The movement of the spheres causes the change in the universe. Each sphere causes the one inside it to move, until you get to the outermost sphere, which has to be moved by something which is not itself moved (or it would need an explanation for its own movement). This is called the **PRIMUM MOBILE** or the **PRIME MOVER**

- **CAUSE OF MOTION** - The object of desire moves other things without itself moving (think of how a saucer of milk draws a cat to it). In this way the prime mover is the cause of the motion of all other things

- **FINAL NOT EFFICIENT CAUSE** - The Prime Mover is immaterial and is the teleological cause of the universe

- **DRAWN IN** - All things are being drawn to it, as to their own final end

- **IMMUTABLE** - The Prime Mover is unchanging and unaffected by anything

- **CONSEQUENCES OF IMMUTABILITY** - Because of its immutability it is therefore everlasting, impassive and necessary

Evaluation of the Prime Mover

The Aristotelian idea of the Prime Mover profoundly affected the notion of God that the Church developed. In particular scholastic theologians such as Aquinas blended scripture with Aristotle and Plato's ideas of God, and arrived at an immutable, impassible, eternal, immaterial and necessary being. The problem is that there is a great tension between the God of scripture and the God of philosophy. Some problems:

- If God is immutable then why bother praying to Him?

- If God is unaware and unaffected by the world, what do we make of the scriptural passages in which He takes an active interest in the world

- If God is unaware of the world, then how can He know everything that will happen (omniscience)?

Some answers might be:

- Prayer does not change God, it changes the one praying

- God in Himself is unchanging, but through his immanent aspect (the Logos or Spirit) he takes an interest in all things

- God is not the same thing as the Prime Mover - Aquinas makes crucial adjustments to the idea to fit with scripture. Eg. For Aristotle God is pure Being, but for Aquinas what this essentially means is pure overflowing love - all being is being-for-another, and the relationship of God in the Trinity cannot be reduced to Aristotelian ideas

- In other words Greek philosophy alone is insufficient for an understanding of God - we need revelation and especially the Trinitarian revelation that we find throughout scripture

The Prime Mover versus The Form of the Good

▸ Similarities

- **BOTH LINKED** - Both are linked in the domain of ethics. The Prime Mover through the idea of everything being drawn to its own purpose, and the form of the Good as the means by which everything that exists is known

- **BOTH ULTIMATES** - They are both "ultimates" which might appeal to non-theistic deists – impersonal sources of reality, arrived at through philosophical speculation, rather than faith

- **BOTH EXEMPLARS** - They have both served as exemplars for a way of explaining the world in terms of a "theory of everything" - arguably without them, science as we know it could not have developed

▸ Differences

- **ARGUMENTS** - The Prime Mover is based on arguments that appeal to **A POSTERIORI** evidence, the form of the Good on A PRIORI arguments

- **IMMANENT** - The Prime Mover is immanent - ie. within the world, whereas the Form of the Good is **NON-SPATIAL** and **NON-TEMPORAL**

- **MORE EXPLANATORY** - The Prime Mover has more explanatory power than the Form of the Good, which is posited as the source of all good things

Rationalism or Empiricism?

- **SENSES** - How dependent on our senses are we for knowledge? How you answer this question will largely form your assumptions about rationalism and empiricism.
- **EMPIRICAL SUPERIORITY** - Empiricists argue that sense experience is the ultimate source of knowledge. They have heavy intuitive support for this from our everyday experience - we know that we rely to a great deal on our senses to get around
- **INDEPENDENT CONCEPTS** - However, rationalists argue that concepts are independent of sense-experience, in that no matter how much sense-data you have, that can never in itself constitute knowledge - some kind of analytical function has to occur, which is not in itself

simply the accumulation of more data

- **EPISTEMOLOGICAL** - Therefore it is a debate in the field of epistemology (philosophy of knowledge)
- **SCEPTICISM** - **HUME** (empiricist) said that ideas do not exist in themselves independently from objects, other than as a relation between objects. For instance, see Hume's Fork

However, there are good arguments for the existence of non-empirical rational objects, for instance the argument from ontological commitment, which might reinforce rationalist or Platonic arguments.

NEED MORE HELP ON ARISTOTLE?

Use your phone to scan this QR code

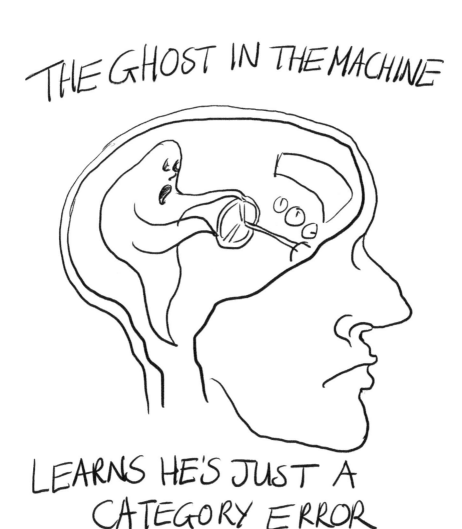

THE GHOST IN THE MACHINE

LEARNS HE'S JUST A CATEGORY ERROR

The Nature of Soul, Mind and Body

In this chapter we will examine different views on identity, awareness and the nature of mind. In particular we will look at the different arguments people have given for a belief in a non-material substance (sometimes called mind or soul) as well as a material substance (body). Some philosophers have argued that the concept of a non-material substance is incoherent, and that the facts can be explained by a monist materialist view (that there is only one substance which is matter, and that mind is ultimately based on this).

KEYWORDS

- **WILL** - Faculty of self-determination, ability to direct one's self as one wishes

- **APPETITE** - Desires or passions

- **REASON** - Faculty of cognition including power to think and form judgements logically

- **BLUEPRINT** - Master plan or overview - template

- **DUALISM** - Belief in two substances

- **MONISM** - Belief in one substance

- **MECHANISTIC** - Describing explanations which argue in reductive or materialistic terms

- **MATERIALISM** - Belief that reality is composed of the one substance of matter

- **EXTENSION** - Spreading-out in space

- **CARTESIAN DUALISM** - Term for Descartes' type of substance dualism

- **EMPIRICAL** - Reasoning based on data gathered from sense experience

- **GHOST IN THE MACHINE** - Ryle's term for the category mistake of assuming non-material explanations for objects which can be explained in material/behavioural terms

- **CATEGORY MISTAKE** - An error of thinking

- **PHILOSOPHICAL BEHAVIOURISM** - A theory of mind that mental concepts can be explained in terms of behavioral concepts

- **QUALIA** - A quality as experienced by a person, eg. the smell of fresh-baked bread

- **INTENTIONALITY** - The quality of mental states which consists in their being directed towards some object or state of affair

- **CONSCIOUSNESS** - State or quality of awareness

- **ROMANTICISM** - Movement in literature and the arts which rejected enlightenment rationalism and emphasised inspiration and subjectivity

PLATO'S VIEW OF THE SOUL

From the **ANALOGY OF THE CAVE** and the **THEORY OF FORMS** it can be seen that for Plato the soul is a non-material essence.

The **CHARIOTEER ANALOGY** helps to understand the tripartite (threefold) nature of the soul: Two horses (**WILL** and **APPETITE**) are controlled by the charioteer (**REASON**). Plato believed that unless the charioteer keeps control on the reins, the will (the weaker horse) will be dragged in the direction that the appetite (the stronger horse) wants to go.

Plato was a **DUALIST** and believed that the soul is deformed through its association with the body. The soul is separable from the body, and as it is non-material, is in a sense indestructible

PLATO'S ARGUMENTS FOR THE SOUL

- **THE CYCLICAL NATURE OF EXISTENCE** - As sleep follows waking, so waking follows sleep, and as death follows life, so life follows death

- **THE ARGUMENT FROM KNOWLEDGE** - Plato claims we have innate knowledge by which to make comparisons, which can only come from the world of the Forms – therefore our souls pre-existed our physical bodies in this world

Since it is the soul and not the body that grasps the Forms, then the soul must belong to that world too. In that case it is unchangeable and indivisible, just as the Forms are.

ARISTOTLE'S VIEW OF THE SOUL

Aristotle had an entirely different view of the soul. The soul is the **FORM OF THE BODY**.

For Aristotle, the form of something is related to the cause, specifically the formal cause, which is the **BLUEPRINT** or map of something.

The form of something is found in its functioning

The form of the car, for example, is found through the combustion of petrol, the action of the engine and the movement of the wheels. In other words, the working-together of all the processes of the car.

In that sense, you cannot say that you have a BMW if all you have is a pile of BMW parts: They have to be connected together and functioning in the manner intended.

Equally, even if you have a collection of human parts, unless they all function together you cannot say that there is a soul or form of human there.

The soul is inseparable from the body

It follows from the above that, in contrast to Plato's dualist position, Aristotle does not hold that the soul is separable from the body - that when the body dies, you cannot meaningfully speak of a form or soul of the body because decomposition begins.

An analogy to this is that of the eye - Aristotle says the soul of the eye is the sight. If the eye is not functioning there is no sight, and equally if the body is not functioning there is no soul.

Or another way Aristotle gives is the wax and the seal. When heated wax is imprinted with someone's seal or stamp (to seal an official letter for instance) it is impossible to separate the imprint of the seal from the wax itself. In this way the form of the body, the soul, is imprinted on it, but is also inseparable from the working of the body itself.

METAPHYSICS OF CONSCIOUSNESS

Descartes' Substance Dualism

Descartes' (1596-1650) was a French philosopher, mathematician and scientist who has had a major influence on western thought. He arrived at his position on the soul as a result of a profound scepticism about what it was possible to know. He is famous for his thought experiment:

- **DEMON DECEPTION** - An evil demon deceives you into believing that the evidence of your senses is real, but in fact it is entirely illusory

- **CANNOT BE CERTAIN** - How do you know for sure that this is not the case? The point is that you cannot entirely be certain that this is not true

- **THERE MUST BE A YOU** - However, even if you assume that there is a deceiver, it follows from the fact of you being deceived that there is a "you" - that much is certain

- **THINKING IS REAL** - Whilst you can be deceived about the content of thoughts (eg. that there is a world which is presented to your senses), you cannot be deceived that you are a thinking subject that seems to perceive things

In other words, there needs to be a subject - **YOU** - who is the subject of the deception.

Descartes frames this as **COGITO ERGO SUM** or;

 "I think therefore I am"

So we can have certainty that there is a mental substance or "thinking", and we can be sure that that is not the same as matter. How can we be sure of this?

By application of **LEIBNIZ' LAW OF IDENTITY** (if two things are the same thing they must share all the same properties)

The argument here goes:

- **I CAN BE SURE THAT MY MIND EXISTS** - See the evil demon experiment

- **I CANNOT BE SURE THAT MY BODY EXISTS** - See above, again

- **MIND AND BODY MUST BE TWO SEPARATE SUBSTANCES** - By application of Leibniz' Law, they must be two separate substances because, if they were the same thing we would be able to be certain the body existed as well

So Descartes has arrived at the conclusion that mind and body are not the same thing. In fact, Descartes says that the key difference is that matter (body) is extended in space (he calls it **RES EXTENSA**) and mind is unextended (he calls it **RES COGITANS**).

This echoes Plato's earlier dualism in which the soul (mind) is essentially non-material and indivisible.

Evaluation

▸ **Weaknesses**

- **MAJOR FLAWS** - There are major flaws with Descartes' theory. Firstly, he fails to give a coherent account of how mind and body interact, when one is physical and spatial and the other non-physical and non-spatial.

- **PINEAL GLAND** - Descartes claimed that the two interacted via the pineal gland in the brain, but this is speculative

- **FROM WITHIN** - As we will see, Leibniz' law is not necessarily applicable to the difference between mind and body, as it may be that the supposed difference in properties is the result of viewing our consciousness from within (see next point)

- **MASKED MAN FALLACY** - Descartes' use of Leibniz' Law of Identity unfortunately falls foul of the Masked Man fallacy - If you saw a masked man at a party, and someone told you it was your father, if your response was 'that can't be my father; it looks nothing like him' then you would be making a major mistake. The same thing applies to Descartes' argument - he has not shown that mind and body actually have different properties, only that his perception of their properties differs in each case

- **CARTESIAN DUALISM** - Is Platonic in a sense as it is dualist, but the moral dimension of Plato's dualism has been lost - Descartes' dualism is **MECHANISTIC** - matter becomes nothing more than extension in space, and soul becomes pure spirit, devoid of any ethical character. This paves the way for the manipulation of physical forces by science and technology, and is a step on the road to the **DISENCHANTMENT** of the modern world where atheistic positivism holds sway.

▶ **Strengths**

- **SUBSTANCE DUALISM EASIER TO EXPLAIN** - Substance dualism does account for some features of consciousness that materialism finds difficult to explain:

- **QUALIA** - Qualities as experienced are one of these features. The problem of accounting for qualia is called by David Chalmers the "hard problem of consciousness"

- **EXPLANATORY GAP** - That is, why does the experience of the smell of fresh-cut grass have the form that it does, and not some other? Even if we can trace the chemicals which create the smell, we are no closer to explaining why it smells the way it does - this is known as the explanatory gap

- **DUALISM & DESCARTES** - We will see that such properties, inasmuch as they make materialism less plausible, provide support for dualism, and thus Descartes

MATERIALISM

Materialism is the belief that there is one substance which is matter and everything else is reducible to it, including mind.

As we have seen, modern materialism was partly made possible by the effect of **CARTESIAN DUALISM** on western thought. If matter is mere extension, and mind is non-spatial, then it is simple to bracket off mind and focus purely on the physical substance.

Arguments for materialism based on **EMPIRICAL** critiques of mind/soul/dualism:

Ryle's Philosophical Behaviourism

GILBERT RYLE calls Descartes' theory "the ghost in the machine" where **GHOST = MIND** and **MACHINE = BODY**. According to Ryle, there is no mind which exists as a separate entity to the body, and to search for one was to make a **CATEGORY MISTAKE**.

By this he means that brain and mind belong to different **LOGICAL CATEGORIES**, but have mistakenly been associated together.

One analogy for this is his story of the foreigner who, visiting Cambridge or Oxford University for the first time, is shown all the different colleges and buildings, but then asks "But where is the University?"

The mistake is that he is still looking for something separate from all the buildings he has been shown, without realising that he has already seen the university.

In just the same way, Ryle argues, dualists are mistakenly searching for something over and above the brain, or behaviour, called the mind.

Ryle was a **PHILOSOPHICAL BEHAVIOURIST** who saw "mental" events as just referring to a specific pattern of behaviour - "mind" is no longer internal; it is what we do with our bodies.

For example, when someone is depressed or angry or joyful, we look at the pattern of behaviour they exhibit in each different case and we cannot see beyond this behaviour. So **MENTAL TERMINOLOGY** actually means something physical, for example, **BEHAVIOUR**.

Evaluation

Counter-intuitive to humans as subjects who have what they perceive as internal states of mind, some of which may not manifest as outward patterns of behaviour at all - do they not exist?

Ryle partly anticipates problematic states such as wishing, which seems to have no particular pattern of behaviour attached to it, by talking about **DISPOSITIONS TO BEHAVE**.

Appropriate behaviour is regarded as potential, and can be anticipated given certain circumstances. So, a person wishing to go on holiday may spend much time on travel websites, for instance.

Ward feels Ryle's account is inadequate:

- **PRETENDING** - Firstly, what about pretending? Someone who pretends to be angry and someone who is angry may exhibit the exact same behaviour, but one of them is not experiencing the same internal state.

- **RECOGNITION** - Secondly, as mentioned, we do know our experience from the inside, and when we feel pain for instance we know that such a feeling cannot be completely captured by a description of the way we behave when we feel it.

- **SELF-AWARE** - Thirdly, what about self-awareness? It is impossible to say how being aware of yourself as a thinking being is capable of being described in terms of behaviour or a **DISPOSITION TO BEHAVE** in a certain way.

IDENTITY THEORY

MIND-BRAIN IDENTITY is another model for the materialist explanation of **CONSCIOUSNESS**.

Although we have different words for mental events and the physical processes which underlie them, they are the same, really. For example, talk of the **EVENING STAR** and the **MORNING STAR** seems to be about two different objects - but they both refer to the same thing - the planet Venus.

Neurologists are able to point to **FMRI SCANS** which correlate some mental states with certain patterns of activity. However, it is easy to oversimplify this and many mental states involve many different parts of the brain.

Evaluation

There are clearly some key aspects of mental states that it is very difficult to explain, if they are identical to brain states.

For instance, **QUALIA** and **INTENTIONALITY**:

- **QUALIA** - These are felt experiences like smelling freshly-cut grass. They are properties of the world as seen from the subjective perspective, and cannot be seen from the "outside-looking-in"

- **INTENTIONALITY** - This describes the fact that thinking is about something, one's attention is directed towards something

Both of these properties of **CONSCIOUSNESS** seem to point to something that current materialist theories are unable to account for; after all it is hard to see how even very complex arrangements of physical "stuff" can give rise to the felt experience of tasting a hamburger.

However, Dennett says that consciousness is "a bunch of tricks in the brain", and that although it is tempting to think so, we are not experts on our own thinking, and that our minds are constantly fooling us. This means that we must be wary of assuming things like qualia cannot be explained without positing MIND.

DAWKINS ON SOUL ONE AND SOUL TWO

The biologist **RICHARD DAWKINS** has become famous for his writing on the subject of religion and science. He has said that we can discern two definitions of soul - the classical notion of soul as a non-material essence of humans, and a more modern romantic version of the soul as metaphor, a way of imaginatively experiencing the world.

The soul as metaphor:

- **SOUL AS A METAPHORICAL REALITY** - The Romantics opened up a way of understanding the soul as a metaphorical reality for the faculty which appreciates the sublime aspects of nature and existence.

- **PLATONIST DUALISTS** - However, they were influenced by Thomas Taylor's translations of Plato's works, and it is clear that many of the Romantics were essentially Platonist dualists.

- **DAWKINS** - In recent times Dawkins has called the poetic notion of soul as an **AESTHETIC SENSE** within us "soul two", which he contrasts with soul one - the traditional non-material essence.

- **SOUL TWO** - The concept of soul two, or soul as metaphor, is only soul in a weak sense, and is not a challenge or threat to a materialistic worldview.

- **ABILITY TO REACT** - Soul in this sense is just an ability to react with awe or wonder at the natural world.

- **NO PLATONIST** - So Dawkins has dropped the Platonism from the concept, and kept the poetic appreciation of the natural world.

- **NOT TWO TYPES OF SOUL** - In no sense does Dawkins believe there are two types of soul - he is using "soul one" and "soul two" as a way of showing that we should drop the classical idea of soul as non-material.

- **SCIENCE HAS KILLED SOUL ONE** - He says that science "has killed or is killing" this idea of soul.

NEED MORE HELP ON THE NATURE OF SOUL, MIND AND BODY?

Use your phone to scan this QR code

Arguments about the Existence or Non-existence of God

Arguments for the existence of God are part of what is known usually as Natural Theology, which is contrasted with Revealed Theology. In your Developments in Christian Theology module you will look in more detail at these. In this module we examine reasons based on sense-data, as well as reasons based on logic alone.

KEYWORDS

- **QUINQUAE VIAE** - Aquinas' Five Ways - arguments for God's existence

- **A POSTERIORI** - Describing arguments which use sense data to support their conclusion

- **ORDER** - Structure, non-chaos

- **COMPLEXITY** - Not simple, intricate or complicated

- **PURPOSE** - Goal or aim

- **EPICUREAN HYPOTHESIS** - Theory of Epicurus that given everlasting time, all possible combinations of atoms will occur

- **EVOLUTION** - Change in the heritable characteristics of biological populations over successive generations

- **COSMOLOGICAL ARGUMENT** - That the universe needs an explanation

- **NECESSITY** - The state of being required

- **PRINCIPLE OF SUFFICIENT REASON** - Principle that states that everything must have a total not partial reason

- **FALLACY OF COMPOSITION** - When one infers that something is true of the whole from the fact that it is true of some part of the whole

- **FORMAL FALLACY** - A pattern of reasoning rendered invalid by a flaw in its logical structure

- **INFORMAL FALLACY** - An invalid pattern of reasoning which is not formally fallacious

- **NECESSARY BEING** - Being which cannot not exist

- **VALID** - True by virtue of its logical form

- **ONTOLOGICAL ARGUMENT** - A priori argument for God

- **TTWNGCBC** - Acronym to help remember key part of Anselm's argument (That Than Which Nothing Greater Can Be Conceived)

- **PREDICATE** - Something which is affirmed or denied concerning an argument

ARGUMENTS BASED ON OBSERVATION

Arguments based on observation (a posteriori arguments) occupy a prominent place in the philosophy of religion. Thomas Aquinas in his Summa Theologiae set out five arguments known as the Five Ways or **QUINQUAE VIAE**. They are all a posteriori, as he did not believe an a priori argument for God would be valid. The first argument we will examine is actually the fifth of Aquinas' Five Ways.

Teleological argument (Aquinas' Fifth Way)

Teleological derives from the Greek word telos, meaning goal or purpose. The world and things in it seem to move towards certain goals or ends, so nature is viewed as directed. Teleological arguments go all the way back to Plato, who proposed that the cosmos is directed by intelligence.

Aquinas' fifth way makes use of the observation that non-intelligent organic life acts in certain ordered, cyclical and purposive ways. Eg. Acorns, given the right conditions, always grow into oak trees and not wombats; the moon has a regular 29 and a half day cycle, etc. Given that non-intelligent things such as acorns and plankton always act in certain ways for certain goals, implies that they were given those goals by an intelligence, because only intelligent beings are able to assign a purpose to things, and move that thing towards its purpose.

Aquinas gives the example of arrows fired by an archer to hit a target. Without the purposive direction imparted by the archer, the arrow would remain in the quiver. The argument relies on an Aristotelian notion of causes, especially final cause. His argument is often referred to as **QUA REGULARITY** (relating to regularity), because Aquinas is pointing to things which always occur in the same regular way to achieve the same end.

A simplified version of the argument might say that the order and purpose we see in the universe needs an explanation in terms of a guiding intelligence.

The argument can be put like this:

- The natural world obeys natural laws

- Natural things flourish as they obey these laws

- Things without intelligence can't direct themselves

- Therefore, things without intelligence require something with intelligence to direct them to their goals

- This is God

William Paley's Teleological Argument

Paley argues from order and complexity to design. His argument consists of two parts: the first is called design **QUA PURPOSE** (relating to purpose). Paley sets out an analogy in the form of a story:

- Walking across a heath, someone finding a rock would not need to ask the question as to how the rock got there - they would assume natural causes.

- But if someone found a watch on the heath, the previous answer would not work - that the watch had always been there - they would assume a designer.

- This is because of the complexity and the purpose inherent in the watch - it has been put together in a complex manner in order to tell the time - all the parts work together for that purpose, and it shows evidence of workmanship.

- If any of the parts were put together in a different way, the watch wouldn't work, which strongly implies all the parts were assembled purposefully in the right order.

- This must have been done by a designer, not by sheer chance.

Paley goes further and anticipates objections:

- Even if the watch sometimes goes wrong, this still implies it was designed for a purpose.

- We would be even more impressed with the watchmaker if the watch could produce more watches.

- Therefore, the design of the watch implies the presence of intelligence and design.

Paley goes on to look at things in the natural world which imply the evidence of design, such as the human eye, the wings of birds and the fins of fish. These are all examined in terms of design.

The second part of Paley's argument is design **QUA REGULARITY**:

- **ASTRONOMY** - He uses evidence from Astronomy, Newton's laws of motion and gravity to point to design in the universe

- **ROTATION** - He points to the regular rotation of the planets

- **DESIGN** - All of this regularity points to design

Assessing the arguments

- **BOTH ARGUMENTS** - Both arguments "beg the question". Aquinas assumes all things need a designer in order to conclude that God designed everything, Paley gives the example of a watch, something which we know has been designed, as an analogy for the world, whose design is the thing in question

- **HUME** - Analogy can only compare similar things, the watch is not similar to the universe. As the universe seems organic, why not compare something organic, like a cabbage?

- **UNIQUE UNIVERSE** - The universe is not like all the other things we can experience

- **MULTIPLE DESIGNERS** - A watch has many designers usually so, why not the universe?

- **EPICUREAN HYPOTHESIS** - The universe could have come about randomly and still look designed, given enough time, which is called the Epicurean hypothesis

- **MORAL DESIGNER** - The presence of evil and suffering in the universe prompts us to ask what kind of designer it has. For example, Dawkins' Digger Wasp

The Challenge of Evolution

There are some major challenges that Darwin's theory of evolution has thrown up against the design argument. Here are the most important:

- **RANDOM CHANGES** - These can lead to order and complex systems can be self-arranging. This is the upshot of the nature of evolution, in which organisms which adapt to their environments are able to pass on their genes more effectively than ones that can't. Thus, there is no need to appeal to a divine intelligence to account for complexity and "order". They arise "naturally" from the processes of evolution and natural selection.

- **DAWKINS & ATKINS** - Point to profound suffering and cruelty in the way the processes of evolution work. The female digger wasp for instance lays her eggs in a caterpillar so that the larva can eat the insides as they grow; she also stings it to paralyse it so it is alive as they are eating it.

- **EVOLUTION** - Challenges the Aristotelian account of causation which includes telos or purpose, as it shows that natural processes can be explained without the need to refer to a goal.

THE COSMOLOGICAL ARGUMENT

This argument is so titled because it usually refers to the **PRESENCE OF THE COSMOS AS EVIDENCE FOR GOD** - not the nature of the cosmos - that is what design arguments do. It asks the question:

"Why is there something rather than nothing?"

Aquinas' Three Ways

The classic formulations of the cosmological argument can be found in **AQUINAS' 3 WAYS**, but these have their roots in Aristotelian philosophy. In fact if you understood how and why Aristotle arrived at his Prime Mover, then you should have no problem with this argument.

▸ Aquinas' 1st Way

Objects in the Universe:

- **ARE POTENTIALLY MOVING** - All things are potentially moving. In other words, they can change into something else in the way that an acorn can change into an oak

- **MOVE FROM ONE STATE TO ANOTHER** - All things require something actual to move them from their state of potentiality. For example, a stick is potentially on fire and only becomes "actually" on fire when a flame is applied to it

- **CANNOT MOVE THEMSELVES** - From a state of potential to actual, meaning everything requires something else to move it, but you must have a first mover which is not moved itself to be the cause of the movement of other things (if you did not, there would be no explanation for the movement of the things which are currently in motion, because you cannot keep going back forever in the chain of movement)

- **REQUIRE A FIRST MOVER** - This first mover which imparts motion to other things but which is not moved is called God

▸ Aquinas 2nd Way

Objects in the Universe:

- **SELF-PERPETUATE** - All things are caused by other things

- **CANNOT REPRODUCE ALONE** - Nothing can be the cause of itself

- **REQUIRE AN INITIAL CAUSE** - You cannot keep going back in the series of causes forever, or you would have no things now. In other words, if there was no initial cause, there could not be other causes. There must be a first cause, itself uncaused, which began the causes

- **ARE CAUSED BY GOD** - This is what people call God

▸ Aquinas' 3rd Way

Objects in the Universe:

- **ARE CONTINGENT** - All things can possibly not exist

- **CAME FROM NOTHING** - If time is infinite, there must have been a point when there was nothing

- **WOULD STILL BE NOTHING** - If there was nothing once, there would be nothing now

- **REQUIRED SOMETHING** - There must be something that is necessary (impossible not to exist)

- **WERE NECESSARY** - Everything that is necessary is either caused by another necessary thing or not

- **ARE UNIQUE** - You cannot have an infinite series of such causes

- **WERE CAUSED BY NECESSITY** - There must be an uncaused necessary being

- **ARE CAUSED BY GOD** - This is what people call God

HUME'S CRITICISMS OF ARGUMENTS FROM OBSERVATION

What Does David Hume Say?

- **NO EXPERIENCE** - We have no experience of universes being made, so we cannot claim to know what caused this one

- **INFINITE REGRESS** - It may be that an infinite regress is possible - see oscillating universe hypothesis

- **UNIVERSE NECESSARY** - It may be that the universe itself is necessary

- **WHY ASSUME?** - Why assume that the necessary thing is a being, or even a being called God?

Teleological Argument

- **POOR ANALOGY** - Analogies are stronger the more alike the two things being compared are. In the case of the design argument Hume claims that the world and the watch are very unlike each other. The world is composed of organic and mineral matter, so it is not like a machine, and more like an organism.

- **MANY GOVERNING PRINCIPLES** - Hume says that the governing principle of the world could be one of many such as generation or gravity, and that these would work equally as well as intelligence. There might not even be one supreme governing principle, but many, each in charge of their own domain.

- **BEGS THE QUESTION** - The analogy of a man-made thing is bound to lead to the conclusion that the universe was designed, but Hume points out that we already have experience or knowledge of watches or houses being made, and so this just begs the question when it comes to the universe.

- **ANTHROPOMORPHISM** - Also, the analogy of a man-made thing implies a human-like God (like effects imply like causes), but this causes problems as God is meant to be infinite in His qualities: A perfect God cannot be inferred from the state of the universe; as Hume says:

"The world is very faulty and imperfect, and was only the first rude essay of some infant deity who abandoned it"

- **MORALITY** - Analogy leads to a non-moral God. One should judge the craftsman on the quality of the work they produce. Earthquakes and illness do not imply a just God. There could be two gods or forces, a good and an evil. That would explain far better the state of the universe.

Cosmological Argument

Hume attacks the principle of **SUFFICIENT REASON** on which the 3rd Way is founded. This principle states that there should be a total explanation rather than a partial one for any phenomenon. Hume argues that you cannot move from saying individual elements of the universe require an explanation, to the whole universe requiring an explanation. This is to commit the **FALLACY OF COMPOSITION**. The fallacy of composition is to assume that just because all the individual members of a group of things have a certain property, that the group itself will have that property. For instance, just because all the tiles on a floor are square, does not mean that the whole floor has to be square - it could be many other shapes.

However, the fallacy of composition is not a **FORMAL FALLACY** and does not always hold: If you substitute colour for shape in the floor tile example above, it is clear that the fallacy doesn't work (if every floor tile is red, then the whole floor **WILL** be red).

So the question is whether contingency is a property more like shape or colour in the floor tile analogy. It certainly seems difficult to see how if everything in the universe is dependent on other things for its existence, how the universe as a whole could not also be dependent on something else for its existence.

Hume questions the **REALITY OF THE WHOLE** that people refer to, saying that "whole" things are usually created by "arbitrary acts of the mind". Eg. when we unite several counties into one kingdom, this has no influence on the nature of things, it is simply a human perception.

The word **UNIVERSE** could be just a convenient term for our own perceptions, rather than referring to any reality. Modern physics would seem to provide some support for this with the view of **POCKET**

UNIVERSES that exist within larger ones - to look for a "whole" gets very difficult in this view.

Hume says that it is not inconceivable that the world had no cause, or just always existed. He says "it is neither intuitively or demonstratively certain" that every object that begins to exist owes its existence to a cause.

He also says that **LIKE CAUSES PRODUCE LIKE EFFECTS**. This seems to be true in the case of parent rabbits producing baby rabbits, for example, so as many things in the universe seem to be the offspring of two parents, why should we assume that there is one male "parent" of the universe. Wouldn't it make more sense to postulate a male and female creator God?

To base an argument on causation would be foolish, as we could never be sure that causation is anything other than a psychological effect. In fact it would be even more foolish in the case of the universe, because lacking past experience of formation of universes, we haven't even got anything to base our "habit of mind" on.

Any being that exists can also not exist, and there is **NO CONTRADICTION** implied in conceiving its non-existence, but this is exactly what would have to be the case, if its existence were necessary. So the term **NECESSARY BEING** makes no sense a posteriori. Any being claimed to exist may or may not exist. In Hume's own words "All existential propositions are synthetic."

ARGUMENTS BASED ON REASON

Arguments based on reason are **VALID A PRIORI**, without the need to refer to observations from experience; they are simply logically true in the same way that the argument:

All men are mortal ➜ Socrates is a man ➜ Therefore Socrates is mortal

Is logically true. A priori arguments are true by definition, in the same way that 2+2=4 is true by definition because another way of defining 2+2 is to call it 4. If it can be shown that God exists by definition then a priori arguments would work.

▸ The Ontological Argument

The argument is known in different forms. The generally accepted classical formulation is from Anselm (1033-1109). It is found in chapters 2-4 of his work Proslogion . The logical demonstration in the argument either totally succeeds or totally fails - it is a **LOGICAL DEDUCTIVE ARGUMENT**.

▶ Anselm's Argument (1st form)

God is that than which nothing greater can be conceived - **TTWNGCBC**.

Even the atheist can have this definition in his understanding.

But if he has it in his understanding (ie in the mind) only, then there must be a greater being who exists both in the mind and reality (it is greater to exist both in the mind and reality).

Therefore, by the definition **TTWNGCBC**, God must exist both in the mind and in reality.

Another way of saying this is that it is self-contradictory to be capable of conceiving something than which nothing greater can be thought, and at the same time to deny that that something really exists.

▶ Anselm's Argument (2nd form)

The second form of the argument is developed to show the impossibility of conceiving of God as not existing. God cannot not be. Any lesser form of existence where it was possible not to be, would not fit with the definition of God:

- God is **TTWNGCBC** (see 1st form)

- It is greater to be a necessary being than a contingent being

- If God exists only contingently it would be possible to imagine a greater being who exists necessarily

- But if God is **TTWNGCBC** then that being has to be God

- God therefore must be a necessary being, and exist in reality

It is important to note that this is logical necessity and not factual necessity (the kind of necessity arrived at in the cosmological argument).

Evaluation

▶ Gaunilo

A monk, contemporary of Anselm argued you could not define things into existence.

Constructed a reductio ad absurdum argument to show the flaw in Anselm's argument:

- Imagine a lost island - the most excellent of all islands

- You can form the idea of this island in your mind

- Therefore, according to Anselm's logic the island must exist in reality

- But this is absurd, and so is Anselm's argument

Anselm replied that islands are contingent things and therefore do not have necessary existence, whereas God does.

▸ Kant

- Kant argued that "It would be self-contradictory to posit a triangle and yet reject its three angles, but there is no contradiction in rejecting the triangle together with its three angles

- In other words, if God exists he must be necessary, but only if. Definitions can only tell us what God would be like if he existed

- Kant says that existence is not a real predicate. It does not give us any information about an object. 'to exist' merely means that an object is actual

- Existence adds nothing to a concept:

  "If we take the subject (God) with all its predicates (eg. all knowledge), and say "God is" or "There is a God", we attach no new predicate to the concept of God ... merely posit it as being an object that stands in relation to my concept. The content of both must be one and the same ... The real contains no more than the merely possible. A hundred real thalers (German coins) do not contain the least coin more than a hundred possible thalers."

NEED MORE HELP ON ARGUMENTS ABOUT THE EXISTENCE AND NON-EXISTENCE OF GOD?

Use your phone to scan this QR code

Religious Experience

What is religious experience? Many people claim to have directly or indirectly experienced God in some way. Research by Alister Hardy has shown that between 25-45% of adults have had an experience of a presence or power beyond themselves.

RICHARD SWINBURNE has given a schema to fit the different kinds of religious experience into, as they vary considerably. A person can seem to perceive God:

- In experiencing a normal non-religious object, for instance, a sunset

- In experiencing an unusual public object, eg. Jesus' resurrection appearances

(these are public)

- In private sensations describable in normal language (eg. Jacob's ladder dream)

- In private sensations not describable in normal language (eg. mystical experiences)

- Without any sensations, but seeing the whole course of experience in the light of God, or being unable to point to any particular thing that made them seem to be experiencing God

(these three are private)

KEYWORDS

- **RELIGIOUS EXPERIENCE** - An experience of a presence or power beyond oneself

- **EXTROVERTIVE EXPERIENCE** - Stace's term for a **PANTHEISTIC** religious experience

- **INTROVERTIVE EXPERIENCE** - Stace's term for a religious experience in which one's sense of self is dissolved in a greater reality

- **THEISTIC** - Related to a personal, loving creator God

- **MONISTIC** - Related to an impersonal divine ultimate, such as Brahman

- **INEFFABLE** - Indescribable in normal language

- **PASSIVE** - James' term for the experience of loss of control during a religious experience

- **NOETIC** - Bestowing insight or wisdom beyond rational understanding

- **TRANSIENT** - Fleeting, over in a short space of time

- **NUMINOUS** - Otto's term for a powerful and awe-inspiring experience of the divine as "other"

- **MYSTERIUM TREMENDUM** - Otto's term for the nature of the numinous experience - a mystery experienced as overwhelming

- **CREATURE-FEELING** - The feeling of being a contingent, created being, brought on by a numinous experience

- **CONVERSION** - A turning-away from past sinful life, and beginning anew with inner certainty of faith

- **REPENTANCE** - Experiencing remorse for one's sins, saying sorry for them

- **METANOIA** - Literally "changing one's mind", a change of heart resulting in changed way of life

- **VERIDICAL** - Truthful in the sense of relating to a real state of affairs

- **PRINCIPLE OF RATIONALITY** - A fundamental assumption of reasoning, without which no such reasoning would be possible

- **PHYSIOLOGICAL** - Relating to the physical body

- **PSYCHOLOGICAL** - Relating to the mind or psyche

- **ASCETIC** - Relating to the strict practices such as fasting which religious people often undertake

MYSTICAL EXPERIENCE

This has been characterised in different ways. It is usually seen as difficult to put into ordinary language. However, some qualities such as an apprehension of ultimate reality, or an experience of the living God, are often used. The experiences often accompanied by feelings of bliss, deep and lasting joy, humility, transformative effect on one's behaviour and relations with others.

Some attempts to classify mystical experiences:

W T Stace

- **EXTROVERTIVE MYSTICAL EXPERIENCES** - The plurality of objects in the world are transfigured into a single living entity

- **INTROVERTIVE MYSTICAL EXPERIENCES** - A loss of identity as a separate individual occurs, and one merges into the divine reality

R C Zaehner

- **THEISTIC MYSTICISM** - Awareness of God in a living relationship

- **MONISTIC MYSTICISM** - Awareness of the soul, Self or consciousness

William James' characteristics of a mystical experience

- **INEFFABLE** - Impossible to put into words

- **NOETIC** - Conveying insights into the nature of reality which transcend normal discursive thought

- **TRANSIENT** - Fleeting, over within a short space of time

- **PASSIVE** - The mystic feels unable to control the experience, feels "taken over" by it

Rudolf Otto

In **THE IDEA OF THE HOLY**, Otto outlines a concept which he calls the **NUMINOUS**. This approach to mystical experience is one which emphasises God's separateness and otherness. Numinous comes from the latin numen, meaning divinity. Otto was trying to convey by it the original sense of awe-inspiring wonder and terror which he believed lay at the heart of religious experience.

One example is the fear that the disciples felt when Jesus calmed the storm, a supernatural fear, contrasted with their fear of the storm itself, it was a far more profound fear. Another example might be this from Isaiah 6: 1-5:

> "I saw the Lord, high and exalted, seated on a throne; and the train of his robe filled the temple. Above him were seraphim, each with six wings: With two wings they covered their faces, with two they covered their feet, and with two they were flying. [3] And they were calling to one another:
>
> 'Holy, holy, holy is the Lord Almighty

the whole earth is full of his glory.'

At the sound of their voices the doorposts and thresholds shook and the temple was filled with smoke.

'Woe to me!' I cried. 'I am ruined! For I am a man of unclean lips, and I live among a people of unclean lips, and my eyes have seen the King, the Lord Almighty.'"

The characteristic of this experience is the feeling of utter worthlessness, helplessness and dependence experienced by the prophet upon seeing the Lord God.

Otto uses two other latin words to explain the numinous:

- **MYSTERIUM** - The experience is in some sense unavailable to ordinary human reason. It is a mystery. Otto wanted to remind us of the "mystery schools" of Ancient Greece, in which neophytes would undergo rituals involving being led into darkness and being forbidden to speak about the initiation.

- **TREMENDUM** - The experience is awe-inspiring, and both attracts us, and makes us feel our own inferiority as mere creatures. Following from this is:

- **CREATURE-FEELING** - Related to the above characteristic, a sense of one's own contingency as a created being in relation to the source of that existence

EXAMPLES OF MYSTICAL EXPERIENCE

St. Teresa of Avila

In The Interior Castle she outlines many types of religious experience. Through mental prayer:

"God gave her spiritual delights: the prayer of quiet where God's presence overwhelmed her senses, raptures where God overcame her with glorious foolishness, prayer of union where she felt the sun of God melt her soul away."

Jan Van Ruusbroec

"There follows the union without distinction. Enlightened men have found themselves

an essential contemplation which is above and beyond reason, and a fruitive tendency which pierces through every condition and all being, and in which they immerse themselves in a wayless abyss of fathomless beatitude where the Trinity of the Divine Persons possess their nature in essential unity. "

Conversion experience

Conversion – turning-towards – is a term usually used to describe the process of someone turning away from past sinful behaviour, and beginning a new life based on faith in God. Repentance, the word used in the Gospels to describe the action of leaving sin behind and beginning a new life in Christ, is translated from a Greek word metanoia, which has the sense of a turning away from sin, a complete and fundamental change of heart. Conversion is thus a foundational element of Christian life. It can be gradual or sudden, but most practising Christians have some experience of it.

Radical examples of conversion can be found in St. Paul and John Wesley:

- **ST PAUL** - Originally called Saul, Paul was a Jew who persecuted Christians until a sudden experience of the risen Christ on the road to Damascus. He described himself as a new man, a new creation.

- **JOHN WESLEY** - Initially aware that he did not have the same faith in a personal saviour that he saw others had, he had a conversion experience in which he felt his heart warmed and felt trust in Christ that he had been saved from his sins.

WILLIAM JAMES examines conversion in the light of his psychological account of the **SICK SOUL** and the "healthy-minded soul". The sick soul is a personality type that is depressive and pessimistic; the healthy-minded soul is conversely optimistic about life. James claims that whilst it can occur to both types, conversion affects the sick soul in a more profound and long-lasting way. We will examine some key claims of James regarding the sick and healthy-minded soul.

THE HEALTHY-MINDED SOUL AND THE SICK SOUL

"The completest religions would therefore seem to be those in which the pessimistic elements are best developed. Buddhism, of course, and Christianity are the best known to us of these. They are essentially religions of deliverance: the man must die to an unreal life before he can be born into the real life."

William James, Varieties of Religious Experience, Lecture 7

Here are the essentials of James' views on the sick soul and conversion. He begins by delineating the healthy-minded attitude to evil. He claims that this is really to minimise the power of evil, and try to evade it. This makes them happier and more well-adjusted than the sick soul, who tends to dwell on and be affected by evil.

James sees certain types of Christianity as more amenable to the healthy-minded view. For instance, in the Catholic sacrament of confession, one can confess one's sins and "walk away from them" in James' words. He contrasts the healthy-minded view with the more pessimistic view of the sick soul, quoting Goethe who said looking back on his life he had found it "nothing but pain and burden". James believed that when faced with the all-embracing blackness of death, the healthy-minded attitude had nothing to offer, and that the sick soul could have a more profound experience of living.

The Once-Born and the Twice-Born

Using this hierarchy, James makes a further distinction between the once-born and twice-born. The former correspond with the healthy-minded soul, and the latter with the sick soul. For example, the Greek religion, almost entirely naturalistic, corresponds with the healthy-minded soul, but he claims that the Epicureans and Stoics (Greeks) knew no joys like those religions of the twice-born such as Buddhism and Christianity, in which a process of dying and rising happens psychologically to the believer.

EVALUATION

How should we understand religious experience?

Religious experience can be understood in at least three different ways:

- **UNION** - Firstly, as union with a greater power

- **PSYCHOLOGICAL** - Secondly as a psychological effect such as an illusion

- **PHYSIOLOGICAL** - Thirdly as the product of a physiological effect

Union with a greater power

This would mean the experience was veridical, and therefore does not merely seem to be an experience of God, but actually is an experience of God. The problem is that as the experience is merely subjective and private, how can the person who has it be certain of this?

SWINBURNE formulated his principle of credulity to answer this question.

The principle states that we ought to believe that things are as they seem to be unless we have evidence that we are mistaken. This is an axiomatic principle of rationality which we apply all the time without even considering it in everyday life. Swinburne says:

> *"If you say the contrary - never trust appearances until it is proved that they are reliable - you will never have any beliefs at all. For what would show that appearances are reliable, except more appearances? And, if you cannot trust appearances as such, you cannot trust these new ones either. Just as you must trust your five ordinary senses, so it is equally rational to trust your religious sense."*

So Swinburne's method is the clever one of asking why we make an exception to an axiomatic principle of rationality when it comes to religion.

WILLIAM JAMES also argued for an openness to this sort of interpretation. Using a psychological approach and gathering a large range of testimonies he argued for a **COMMON CORE** to religious experience (see above). His conclusions were:

- **VISIBLE WORLD** - That the visible world is part of a more spiritual universe from which it draws its chief significance

- **TRUE END** - That union or harmonious relation with that higher universe is our true end

- **PRAYER** - That prayer or inner communion with the spirit thereof, be that spirit "God" or "law", is a process wherein work is really done, and spiritual energy flows in and produces effects, psychological or material, within the phenomenal world.

Religion includes also the following **PSYCHOLOGICAL CHARACTERISTICS**:

- **A NEW ZEST** - Which adds itself like a gift to life, and takes the form either of lyrical enchantment or of appeal to earnestness and heroism

- **AN ASSURANCE OF SAFETY** - And a temper of peace, and, in relation to others, a preponderance of loving affections

Mackie says of James:

> *"Even what he classes as genuinely religious experiences (ones which leave 'good dispositions' in the believer) do not intrinsically resist explanation in purely human terms."*

Others such as Dawkins have argued similarly: psychological or physiological explanations are far more likely given the prior improbability of a divine being who interacts with humans.

Psychological effect such as an illusion

Often experiences can deceive us, eg. hallucinations. Some people may be mistaken, and even self-deluding.

Freud thought that we feel helpless, need a father figure and create one unconsciously with religious experience, which helps us satisfy the need for security. Jung believed that archetypes in the collective unconscious can cause religious experience.Just because some people are mistaken or hallucinate, it doesn't mean all religious experience is of this character.

And, just because God appears as a father in the way we need Him, doesn't prove that religious experience is not true. It may be God appears that way because he has placed that deep need in us.

Physiological effects

There are well-documented links between the body and the mind. There are **PSYCHOSOMATIC** factors in some illnesses, such as psoriasis and high blood pressure. And the mind can affect things like heart rate, feelings of nausea and so on. As many religious experiences can be subtle, feeling-based, it is possible that physiological factors may be a major cause. Some possible causes include:

- **ASCETIC** - Practices such as fasting can lead to hallucinations etc.
- **PERSINGER HELMET** - This shows how manipulating magnetic fields in the brain can give rise to feelings of a "presence".
- **LIMITED UNDERSTANDING** - We still have a very limited understanding of how the brain works and interacts with physical processes in other parts of the body – it is possible that we will understand religious experiences in natural terms when our knowledge grows.

NEED MORE HELP ON RELIGIOUS EXPERIENCE?

Use your phone to scan this QR code

The Problem of Evil and Suffering

The problem of evil has occupied the thought of theologians for centuries. Many religions and mythologies attempt to account for the existence of evil and suffering in the world - often, as in dualistic worldviews, good and evil gods are at war with each other and this explains the state of the world, split between moments of good and evil, but with neither force ever attaining final triumph. With the advent of monotheism in the revelation to the Israelites a new problem arises. God is the supreme, all-powerful and all-loving God of the universe, and therefore if creation is good, as the Genesis texts say it is, then the existence of evil creates a unique problem. That problem is set out in its two main forms below.

KEYWORDS

- **OMNIPOTENT** - All-powerful

- **LOGICAL PROBLEM** - Description of the problem of evil relating to the coherence of God's attributes and the evil in the world

- **EVIDENTIAL PROBLEM** - Version of the problem of evil relating to sheer amount of evil in the world

- **INDUCTIVE** - Describing the process of induction

- **INSCRUTABILITY** - Unfathomable or unknowable nature of God

- **THEODICY** - Defence of God

- **PRIVATION** - Lack of something which should be possessed by nature

- **EXITUS/REDITUS** - "Going out and coming back"

- **SOUL-MAKING** - Type of theodicy in which suffering leads to growth

- **UNIVERSALISM** - Belief that all will be saved

DIFFERENT VERSIONS OF THE PROBLEM

Logical problem

The logical problem of evil highlights the inconsistency between divine attributes and the presence of evil.

The **INCONSISTENT TRIAD**. First stated by **EPICURUS**, this dilemma can be put like this:

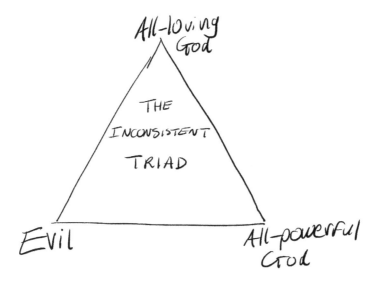

Either God cannot abolish evil, or he will not; if he cannot then he is not all-powerful; if he will not then he is not all-good

The logical form of this can be stated:

- God is **OMNIPOTENT**

- God is **ALL-GOOD**

- God **OPPOSES EVIL**

- Therefore **EVIL DOES NOT EXIST**

Clearly, the conclusion is problematic. Most people would disagree with it. If you disagree with the conclusion, then at least one of the premises must be false.

To deny any of the premises is to deny the God of classical theism:

- **GOD IS OMNIPOTENT** - If you say that He is not all-powerful then you are saying there are things God cannot do. This sounds like it cedes too much ground to the challenge, but most theologians would argue that God's omnipotence is not completely unlimited. In other words, God is not free to do the logically impossible, such as create a square circle, or do an evil act (Aquinas argues that God cannot do this because this would create a lack in God, but as God is perfect he cannot lack any good).

- **NON-INTERFERENCE** - Some would also include God's inability to interfere with human free-will as a self-imposed limitation of God, as part of his loving nature. This is one partial solution to the problem of evil, as we shall see later.

- **GOD IS ALL-GOOD** - This premise is more difficult to get around. If God is not all-good, then we have some mixture of good and evil in God which the main monotheistic religions would deny.

- **GOD OPPOSES EVIL** - God clearly opposes evil, but it might be worth asking in the long-term whether God might allow certain evils to bring about even greater goods. This has also been vigorously debated. See Dostoevsky - The Grand Inquisitor in The Brothers Karamazov for an examination of this question.

The evidential problem of evil

The problem of suffering emphasises a different aspect of the problem of evil. The focus is on the experience of evil, the intensity, and the amount of it. The evidence of so much evil in the world is indeed difficult to explain for the theist.

Whilst arguments from the logical problem of evil aim to show that God's existence is impossible, evidential arguments have the more modest aim of showing that God's existence is unlikely.

Evidential arguments are inductive, in that they point to particular cases of evil in the world.

Most responses to the evidential problem refer to the inscrutability of God's action, and aim to show that God could be justified in allowing the existence of radical evil.

THEODICIES

Augustine

Augustine's use of original perfection and the Fall to justify evil is the classic defence of God or theodicy. It can be presented in steps:

- God is good and made a flawless world "ex-nihilo". (Genesis 1)

- Humans (and angels) were created with free will

- Evil Is created when this free will is used to turn from God to a lesser good

- Evil is "not a substance", but a "privation of good"

- Natural evil is deserved suffering in response to Adam's sin

- Moral evil was the cause of natural evil. Natural evil is a disorder introduced into God's ordered world

Augustine believes that sin is an **ONTOLOGICAL CONDITION** - something that human nature is marked with from the choice of free created beings - angels and humans. The possibility of turning from greater to lesser goods is there in the world both because of free will , and in the way that the world was created by God, in a hierarchical fashion. Some things are better and more valuable than others. Clearly, the theodicy relies on free will: criticisms of it often focus on this and question whether free will can take the weight that Augustine places on it.

Evaluation of Augustine

Modern science rejects the idea of an original perfect state from which we fell. Evolution emphasises the way in which organisms develop from cruder to more complex systems – applied to culture and humanity and morality it implies progress means we are moving away from an original amoral state to an enlightened one. This is clearly highly debatable and many call this the **MYTH OF PROGRESS**.

It seems strange in the modern era to view sin as transferred in a hereditary fashion. Some view this as an outdated idea based on a misunderstanding of biology. For instance, Augustine's claim that we were "all in Adam's loins" reveals a belief that all of the human race was present as seed in Adam's loins and therefore, that all are corrupted by his sin. Needless to say there are many who disagree with such a literal version of the transmission of original sin:

- **PERFECTION** - If humans were created perfect why did they desire to sin? If they did desire to sin, surely that shows they were not created perfect? Couldn't God have created a world where people didn't sin even though they had the possibility of doing so?

- **RESPONSIBILITY** - If God foresaw the evil that would befall and planned to send Christ to redeem the world doesn't that imply some responsibility for evil on God's part?

- **DEBATABLE** - Evil as a privation is debatable and some evil might be characterised as a lack, other evil as an actual presence

- **INCOMPATIBLE** - Augustine's theodicy involves an eternal hell, which seems incompatible with an all-loving God

Is it logically possible for a perfect world to go wrong, and if it is, isn't that ultimately the responsibility of the creator of that world?

Some defences of Augustine

- **MYTHOLOGY** - There is just as much mythologizing involved in placing a "golden age" in the future, as there is in the past. Some would argue that moderns have simply swapped one myth for another.

- **ASPECT OF CUNNING** - Some readings of Genesis interpret the serpent as an aspect of created humanity which is crafty or cunning. In other words, using a gift of God in a way that is less than it is meant to do, to glorify self rather than God and others. This means it is not that God put evil desires in us, rather that freedom means we can choose how to employ our gifts. When we began to systematically employ them in selfish ways, we separated ourselves from God.

- **FREE LOVE** - Love between God and his creatures is only possible if they are free – this means that without freedom we could not share in God's love. Theologians characterise the great gift-giving love of God as **EXITUS AND REDITUS**: a going-out and a returning. Human free will is involved in that return to God, we get to participate in the divine life, which is the flourishing of true freedom.

The Irenaean Theodicy

Found in the writings of **IRENAEUS** (130-202). It is a soul-making theodicy, in that it emphasises the importance of evil and suffering in helping us to develop specific qualities of soul. Evil and suffering therefore play an important role in our salvation. JOHN HICK has developed it in recent times.

GEN 1:26 - Distinguishes between the image and likeness of God. Humans are created in the image of God (ie. they have free will, know good from evil, are capable of rational and moral action and love), but must grow into the likeness of God (actually perform loving actions, choose good and not evil, use free will in the best way), and the only way that this is possible is in a world in which it is significantly possible to turn away from the good. This world is called by **HICK** a **VALE OF SOUL-MAKING** for this reason.

> *"Then God said, 'Let us make mankind in our image, in our likeness, so that they may rule over the fish in the sea and the birds in the sky, over the livestock and all the wild animals, and over all the creatures that move along the ground'. So God created mankind in his own image, in the image of God he created them; male and female he created them."*

Gen 1:26-28

There are therefore two stages which make up the development of humanity:

- **IMAGE OF GOD** - The appearance of humans as the culmination of the evolutionary process
- **MORAL AWARENESS** - The second stage (corresponding to the 'likeness of God') is the dawning of moral awareness in humans and their seeking through religion to love God and neighbour

The **FALL OF HUMANITY** is a failure within this second phase. It is an inevitable part of the maturation process – it helps people to grow and develop.

Hick said the value of this world is:

> *"To be judged, not primarily by the quantity of pleasure and pain occurring in it at any particular moment, but by its fitness for its primary purpose, the purpose of soul-making."*

He argues that God creates people at an **EPISTEMIC DISTANCE** (a distance in knowledge of God) so that they are not compelled to know Him, but must choose to come to know him through an act of faith.

Also, if we do not complete our journey to the likeness of God in this life, we must complete it in the next - but God **GUARANTEES OUR ULTIMATE SALVATION**.

Evaluation of the Irenaean Theodicy

- **UNIVERSAL SALVATION** - This theory is called **UNIVERSALISM**. Some condemn it as unscriptural, and doing away with the need to be moral altogether

- **AUSCHWITZ** - How does suffering like that at Auschwitz justify the **SOUL-MAKING** of individuals? Surely this suffering broke humans rather than perfected them?

- **DYSTELEOLOGICAL EVIL** - Linked to this is the problem of Dysteleological evil - evil that has no purpose. Again the "protest atheism" of Ivan Karamazov which wants no part in God's plan: "I must return my ticket"

- **LEVEL OF SUFFERING** - Do we need such a large amount of suffering to help us develop – gratuitous evil and suffering are a problem for this theodicy

- **WHY PERFECTION?** - Why does God need to use such a long painful process of evolution to perfect humans?

- **OPPORTUNITY** - The theodicy is in keeping with Christian understandings of suffering – that it can be used as an opportunity rather than a limitation. For example, Job

---

NEED MORE HELP ON THE PROBLEM OF EVIL AND SUFFERING?

Use your phone to scan this QR code

Religion and Ethics

(H173/Component 02)

Religious Approaches

Normative Ethical Theories

Applied Ethics

Introducing Religious Ethics

Students entering upon courses of study at A Level and undergraduate level very frequently hold some sort of relativist worldview. One of the strengths of this course is that it will seriously test such a worldview. The relativist view itself is not the problem, rather the unthinking assumption that relativism is the only rational option. As a teacher, I frequently experience "lazy relativism" by students as an excuse not to seriously consider the ideas which challenge their worldview. "The Dude" in the Coen Brothers film "The Big Lebowski" exemplifies this attitude.

Of course, Plato was very clear on the difference between knowledge and opinion. If all we can hold about subjects are opinions based on our own cultural biases which are just as valid as other people's opinions, then we are in trouble, and clearly, very few live their lives on such a basis. Anyway, relativism again falls foul of a self-inflicted undermining. If you can see the problem with this statement you will be aware of the irony: "There is no objective truth apart from the truth that there is no objective truth".

A study of Natural Law in the first year of the course will bring students face to face with an ethical belief-system based on the notion of objective truth revealed by reason. As students usually experience a tension between elements of this system and elements of the postmodern assumptions of contemporary culture, it is important to spend time looking at the philosophical underpinnings of both worldviews. One area where this can be interesting is to look at the institution of marriage from traditional and modern standpoints. Some of the key topics in this module are:

- Natural Law and Eternal Law

- The concept of Telos (purpose)

- The doctrine of Double Effect

- The possibility of Objective Moral Law and relation to subjective judgements

- The applicability of moral judgement to different areas of life

Then as a contrast a relativist, pragmatist approach to Christian ethics is introduced - Situation Ethics. Students get the chance to examine Fletcher's modern take on the Gospel value of agape, or Christian Love. Some key topics here include:

- How useful the concept of agape is

- Whether situation ethics can be said to be "Christian" or religious ethics

- Whether relativism, pragmatism, positivism and personalism are useful

Natural Law

Natural Law is a **NORMATIVE** ethical theory. It has an underlying **TELEOLOGICAL** orientation, and has its origins in the work of Aristotle, but was developed by Aquinas. In other words, a key assumption of Natural Law is that humans by their nature pursue certain **ENDS** which they perceive as good.

KEYWORDS

- **NATURAL LAW** - Normative, teleological ethical theory based on the work of Aristotle, that ethics is based on natural pursuit of rational ends

- **GOOD LIFE** - The belief that there is a rational goal to life, formulated by the ancient Greeks as a life of restraint and civic duty

- **ARISTOTELIAN** - Derived from the thought of Aristotle (384-322 BC)

- **TELOS** - Greek word meaning end or goal

- **TELEOLOGICAL** - Relating to an explanation of a thing in terms of its end or goal

- **MORALITY** - System of beliefs and practices relating to how one ought to live and behave towards others

- **ETERNAL LAW** - According to Aquinas, the law with which God governs the universe

- **DIVINE LAW** - The laws of God which have been revealed to humans, most notably on Mt. Sinai to Moses

- **HUMAN LAW** - Laws which have been derived from human reason alone

- **PRECEPTS** - A specific rule, usually derived from more general principles

- **AXIOM** - An assumption or working principle, not derived from previous arguments, but without which an argument may not be able to be proposed

- **ABSOLUTE** - Having an unchangeable character, not dependent on culture or time

- **RELATIVE/RELATIVISM** - Having a quality in relation to other things, and thus not absolute - time and culture dependent

- **POST-MODERN** - Describing system of thought in which there is no single story or "meta-narrative" about the world - thus relative

- **CONSTRUCTIVISM -** Belief that significant concepts such as number are constructs or human creations, and have no character or meaning beyond the context in which they were created

ORIGINS OF THE CONCEPT OF TELOS IN ARISTOTLE

The notion that the **GOOD LIFE** is one that conforms to the proper ends or goals of humans comes from Aristotle.

Further, that these ends can be discerned through rational reflection on human nature, is an **ARISTOTELIAN** claim.

The idea that **MORALITY** consists in fulfilling one's proper goals, or that the good life is one lived in accordance with our proper ends is a **TELEOLOGICAL** one (**TELOS-** goal or end).

AQUINAS AND NATURAL LAW

In the **SUMMA THEOLOGIAE**, Aquinas develops the notion of a natural law and brings it into a scriptural context, so that it fits with Christian theology. He puts it in the context of more universal laws:

- **ETERNAL LAW** - "The plan by which God, as ruler of the universe, governs all things". All things follow the eternal law in that they "have a tendency to pursue whatever behaviour and goals are appropriate to them".

- **LIMITED UNDERSTANDING** - Human beings, however, follow God's eternal law "in a more profound way". We have a limited understanding of the eternal law, and this means we can use our reason to find out what goals are appropriate for us to follow.

  This planning, both for ourselves and other creatures, is a way of sharing in God's plan. To participate in the eternal law in this way through reason is what Aquinas calls natural law.

- **NATURAL LAW** - The precepts of Natural Law (see below)

- **DIVINE LAW** - Laws revealed by God, for example, the **TEN COMMANDMENTS**, received by Moses on Mt. Sinai. Revealed in scripture, such laws are not necessarily capable of being arrived at by reason alone. They transcend rational discernment, although reason, when used correctly, is not at odds with divine law.

- **HUMAN LAW** - Laws arrived at by a process of rational argumentation, which can supplement the natural law, or specify in more detail what the natural law requires in specific circumstances. Human law should be in accordance with natural law, otherwise it deviates from law understood in its widest sense.

THE PRECEPTS OF NATURAL LAW

Aquinas builds his system of practical reasoning on certain fundamental principles.

One principle is that all practical reasoning depends on a notion of the good. Therefore a basic principle of moral reasoning is that **GOOD SHOULD BE DONE AND PURSUED AND EVIL AVOIDED**.

This is an axiom of **MORAL REASONING**, meaning that it is a self-evident starting point, and it is the key principle of natural law.

There are three **KEY SETS OF GOALS** which Aquinas identifies as good. From his perspective, good means whatever man naturally seeks as a goal.

With these three groups he works out some general moral principles, which are known as **THE PRECEPTS**:

- **GROUP 1** - The basic inclination to go on existing, which all things share, can be seen to be the basis of the moral principle to preserve life.

- **GROUP 2** - The natural tendency which humans and animals share to mate and bring up their young is the next moral principle.

- **GROUP 3** - Distinctively human ends, accessible through reason, are in this group. These are essentially to know the truth about God and to live in society, of which Aquinas gives instances, like shunning ignorance and not offending others.

Notice that these groups progress from general to specific, ie, from all life, to animal and human life, to just humans. This is in line with Aquinas' ideas about vegetative, animal and rational souls, which makes a similar progression.

These groups are often set out as **FIVE PRIMARY PRECEPTS**. These can be set out as:

- **PRESERVATION OF LIFE** - Group 1

- **REPRODUCTION** - Group 2

- **EDUCATION** - Group 2

- **LIVE IN AN ORDERED SOCIETY** - Group 3

- **WORSHIP GOD** - Group 3

The primary precepts can be memorised with the mnemonic **POWER** - **P**reservation, **O**rdered society, **W**orship, **E**ducation, **R**eproduction.

The Secondary Precepts

Each primary precept can be applied to specific situations to produce secondary precepts. These are not as absolute as the primary precepts, and only apply in **CERTAIN SITUATIONS**.

Examples are national laws, which may vary from country to country, eg. laws about marriage, or codes of behaviour that differ in different cultures. For instance, the laws regarding the age of consent or marriage can be as low as 13 in some countries and up to 18 in others. It is a crime in Singapore to chew gum, and heavy fines can be imposed for it, whereas elsewhere, it is not.

The secondary precepts are therefore **REALISTIC** and **FLEXIBLE**.

Apparent Goods

An apparent good is that which merely seems good to us; it satisfies a desire, and is an object of choice, but it is not a true good, as it actually goes against the whole purpose of a human being. Aquinas thinks no-one can seek an evil in and for itself, but everyone is pursuing what they believe is a good for themselves.

As our ultimate purpose is union with God, any good we pursue which ultimately frustrates that purpose cannot be a true good. This means that there are lesser goods, which, when we don't seek to elevate them above their own place, are not a problem. They only become problematic when, due to the disordered nature of our will, we give them undue importance in our lives.

IS NATURAL LAW A HELPFUL METHOD OF MORAL DECISION-MAKING?

Strengths

- **ABSOLUTE & RELATIVE** - It provides both absolute and relative precepts which could be helpful in a variety of situations

- **BASED ON REASON** - Therefore it is accessible to all humans

- **RELEVANT** - The precepts are timeless and relevant to modern society

- **FLEXIBLE** - The secondary precepts help give some flexibility to the system

Weaknesses

- **WHAT IS NATURAL?** - Difficulty deciding on what "natural" is, eg, doctors can prolong someone's life, but does that make it unnatural?

- **KARL BARTH** - A Protestant theologian who rejects use of reason. We should rely on revelation alone to know God's law

- **RELATIVISM CHALLENGE** - The challenge from relativism - does human nature alter over time/culture?

- **THERE IS NO 'NATURE'** - Postmodern/constructivist theory that humans project their own need for order or create narratives to impose order, but that there is none objectively

- **THERE IS NO 'TELOS'** - To the human or the natural world, evolution has dispensed with that idea. We give ourselves our purpose

---

NEED MORE HELP ON NATURAL LAW?

Use your phone to scan this QR code

Situation Ethics

There are ethical theories which claim that utilitarianism is a philosophical version of the Christian command to love your neighbour as yourself. Joseph Fletcher put forward one such theory in situation ethics.

It is a liberal Christian ethical theory

JOSEPH FLETCHER was an American Anglican. He wanted to avoid inflexible versions of Christian ethics which propose absolute rules. Equally he wanted to avoid the opposite extreme of "do what you will".

One way of seeing this is as taking the middle way between **ANTINOMIANISM** and **LEGALISM**.

The only absolute in situation ethics is the command to **LOVE YOUR NEIGHBOUR AS YOURSELF.**

Influenced by **TILLICH**, who said that God is the ground of our being (Tillich's term for God as the ultimate concern of humanity, or that he is more fundamental to our existence than anything else), God is immanent and therefore part of us, so we should not see morality as a set of orders from above, but as a moral law within.

Fletcher says:

"Love's decisions are not made prescriptively, but situationally".

To love your neighbour means to consistently "will and choose the good of the other", in other words, to love what God loves, which is your neighbour's good. In that case we need only work out what will cause his or her good in the situation that he or she is in.

KEYWORDS

- **IMMANENT -** Within the world, in time and space

- **ANTINOMIANISM -** Belief that there are no moral laws that God expects Christians to obey - opposite to legalism

- **LEGALISM -** Belief that obedience to religious law earns salvation

- **AGAPE -** Greek word often translated as Christian or brotherly love

- **PRESCRIPTIVE -** Giving rules or instructions

- **PRAGMATISM -** Belief that a key aspect of truth is if it is productive of positive results, that the meaning of a proposition is found in the practical consequences of accepting it

- **POSITIVISM -** Any system that confines itself to experience and excludes metaphysical theories

- **PERSONALISM -** Belief that the person is central to ethics - and therefore rules/legalism are secondary

- **PAPAL ENCYCLICAL** - A category of letter sent by the Pope to the Catholic faithful

AGAPE

Greek word in new testament meaning **LOVE OF NEIGHBOUR**, deriving from Old Testament Hebrew word **CHESED** meaning mercy

Agape is often translated as Christian love or BROTHERLY LOVE.

New Testament passages which speak of it: **1 JOHN 4:16,21**

> *"God is love. Whoever lives in love lives in God, and God in them. And he has given us this command: Anyone who loves God must also love their brother and sister".*

Agape is embodied in the person of Jesus Christ ("The Word became flesh and dwelt among us")

THE SIX PROPOSITIONS

These give rise to the theory of situation ethics and are fundamental principles focused on the nature of **LOVE** or AGAPE

Situation ethics is a working out of the consequences of these principles, according to Fletcher:

LOVE ...

1. **IS INTRINSICALLY GOOD** - Agape is not about being, but doing; goodness lies in the consequences. Fletcher says you cannot assign good or bad to actions

2. **IS THE RULING NORM -** In ethical decision-making, love is the ruling norm and replaces all laws. Essentially, Fletcher is saying that **LOVE IS THE LAW**, in the sense that love replaces all

laws. So nothing, not even murder, is intrinsically bad if it leads to the most loving outcome

3. **LOVE & JUSTICE ARE THE SAME THING** - Justice is love that is **DISTRIBUTED**. If love is put into practice, it will result in justice. You cannot love someone and allow them to be discriminated against

4. **IS EQUAL** - Love wills the neighbour's good regardless of whether the neighbour is liked or not. There is no favouritism in love, all must be treated equally, even one's enemies. This means we are bound to love others as much as our families

5. **IS ULTIMATE** - Love is the goal or end of the act and that justifies any means to achieve that goal. Love must be the final end of an act, rather than the means to some other goal; we must not be loving to achieve something else

6. **IS SITUATIONAL** - Love decides on each situation as it arises without a set of laws to guide it. Love is therefore situational, not prescriptive; there will not be one set of moral guidelines which covers all situations, but the right thing to do in each situation will be the most loving. This makes it **RELATIVISTIC**

THE FOUR WORKING PRINCIPLES

As well as six propositions about love, Fletcher also gives **FOUR WORKING PRINCIPLES**. Whereas the six propositions were about the nature of love and the consequences for the ethical theory, the four working principles are structural guidelines which situate the system within a wider conceptual framework.

1. **PRAGMATISM** - It is based on experience rather than theory. This is important because Fletcher wants to get away from legalism which can seem remote to people's lived experience. One way of rephrasing pragmatism is "whatever works is the best thing to do". In the context of ethics, this means the best thing to do will be the pathway that produces the most loving outcome.

2. **RELATIVISM** - It is based on making the absolute laws of Christian ethics relative. Everything must be relative to agape, so there is no such thing as a command to "never do" a certain action. **REJECTS TEN COMMANDMENTS**. Notice that agape is absolute, but must be relativised to every situation.

3. **POSITIVISM** - It begins with belief in the reality and importance of love. You have to begin with a positive choice or commitment to love. This is a value judgement, a saying yes to love. Why? Because God is Love. It expresses a belief that love is a feature of the universe.

4. **PERSONALISM** - Persons, not laws or anything else, are at the centre of situation ethics. Similar to Kant's maxim 'treat people as ends, never as means to an end'. Laws take second place to people. God is personal, and wants a personal relationship with us.

Strengths

- **PRAGMATIC** - Many who work in pastoral areas are grateful for an ethical system which can actually be applied to the person in front of them, rather than a set of rules which may not be suitable for that person.

- **LOVE IS CENTRAL** - As it is in the Gospel. This is an essential aspect of situation ethics, which does conform to the greatest commandments as given by Jesus.

- **RELATIVE MEANS FLEXIBLE** - Again, those who work pastorally need a certain flexibility to help them set the person on a pathway back to God - this is often expressed as "meeting people where they are".

Weaknesses

- **'WHATEVER WORKS' IS MORALLY DUBIOUS**- Does pragmatism dispense truth for utility? In other words, as long as I say the right things and act in ways which bring about the most 'loving outcome', then my action is above criticism. But this is to forget that morality has a prescriptive element - value judgements have to be made, in particular the value judgement that can tell what is loving or not.

- **'PERSONS VS RULES' IS FALSE** - Does personalism, in privileging people over laws, create a false dichotomy which risks affirming people in whatever course of action they may be on, regardless of whether it is objectively sinful or not?

CONSCIENCE

According to **FLETCHER**, conscience is not a noun but a verb, a term that describes attempts to make decisions creatively. Fletcher is interested in the reality of love in action and conscience really describes the process of **PUTTING LOVE INTO ACTION**, of willing the good of another.

Fletcher rejects the idea that conscience is intuition, a channel for divine guidance (the voice of God idea), the internalised values of the individual's culture (famously put forward by **FREUD**), or the part of reason that makes value judgements, because all of these try to treat conscience as a thing rather than the process of making decisions creatively.

The Catholic Church rejected situation ethics, not least for the radical departure it makes from the traditional notion of conscience. In the **PAPAL ENCYCLICAL** Veritatis Splendor (1993) Pope John Paul II said:

> *"The relationship between man's freedom and God's law is most deeply lived out in the "heart" of the person, in his moral conscience. As the Second Vatican Council observed: "In the depths of his conscience man detects a law which he does not impose on himself, but which holds him to obedience. Always summoning him to love good and avoid evil, the voice of conscience can when necessary speak to his heart more specifically: 'do this, shun that'. For man has in his heart a law written by God. To obey it is the very dignity of man; according to it he will be judged (cf. Rom 2:14-16)".*

> *"The way in which one conceives the relationship between freedom and law is thus intimately bound up with one's understanding of the moral conscience. Here the cultural tendencies referred to above - in which freedom and law are set in opposition to each other and kept apart, and freedom is exalted almost to the point of idolatry - lead to a "creative" understanding of moral conscience, which diverges from the teaching of the Church's tradition and her Magisterium."*

IS SITUATION ETHICS CAPABLE OF GIVING REAL MORAL GUIDANCE?

Strengths

- **INDIVIDUAL** - Avoids problem of overly rigid inflexible "dogmatic" moral systems which sometimes fail to account for individual situations.

- **FLEXIBLE** - Deontological theories such as Kantian ethics prescribe universal rules which common sense tells us are occasionally inapplicable - situation ethics deals easily with these dilemmas (such as "is it ok to lie sometimes"?).

- **ATTRACTIVE** - Many modern Christians, especially those who work in pastoral areas who need practical applications of Christian ethics which are flexible, find this attractive.

Weaknesses

- **OUTDATED** - Many Christian ethicists regard situation ethics as not having aged well - it is very much from the era of free love and hippies.

- **WEAKNESSES OF CONSEQUENTIALISM** - As it is essentially a form of act-utilitarianism, it suffers from most of the same problems.

- **IT IS TOO THIN** - Lacks a coherent account of the fulness of Christian ethics, and attempts to use a secular philosophical theory to explain a Christian theological system. Some would say it fails to do this adequately.

- **TOO VAGUE** - People need rules to live by.

- **SKIN DEEP** - Despite what Fletcher claims, situation ethics is essentially antinomianism with a veneer of agape to make it palatable to Christians.

- **IMPULSIVE** - Situations do not exist outside of the people in them, who will have their own unconscious or conscious value system which they bring to it. Situation ethics does not stop people acting on impulses or poorly considered values and then retrospectively fitting their actions into an **AGAPEISTIC** framework.

- **UNCERTAINTY** - How can we always know what the most loving thing to do will be? **CHILDRESS** says:

"We cannot say which acts are right or wrong, what we ought to do, until we can say which will probably produce more good than evil but we cannot say which will probably produce more good than evil until we have some conception of value. Situation ethics gives us no help there"

NEED MORE HELP ON SITUATION ETHICS?

Use your phone to scan this QR code

Kantian Ethics

IMMANUEL KANT (1724-1804) was a profoundly influential German philosopher who wrote extensively on ethics. His theory is **DEONTOLOGICAL**, meaning it is concerned with duty, and is absolutist.

KEYWORDS

- **DEONTOLOGICAL** - Ethical system based on deon - Greek for duty - judges morality of action based on whether it has followed rules

- **DIVINE COMMAND THEORY** - System of morality in which morality is divinely revealed, without need for human reason

- **EPISTEMOLOGY** - Theory of knowledge, or study of foundations of how we know

- **NOUMENAL** - Kantian term for world unattainable by human experience - mind-independent

- **PHENOMENAL** - Opposite of noumenal - anything which can be apprehended by senses

- **GOOD WILL** - Faculty of acting according to a conception of law - "the only thing good without limitation" according to Kant

- **HYPOTHETICAL IMPERATIVE** - Any action based on desires, so reason commands it only if it is desired

- **CATEGORICAL IMPERATIVE** - Any action which must be done for its own sake, regardless of whether it is an object of desire

- **CONDITIONAL** - Dependent on factors which might not apply in all cases

- **MAXIM** - A general law or rule of action, often stated in a simple sentence

- **POSTULATE** - A statement accepted as true for the purposes of argument

- **IMMORTALITY** - Inability to die, or ability to live forever

- **SUMMUM BONUM** - The highest good

BACKGROUND TO KANT'S ETHICAL THEORY

Kant's ethics should be understood in the light of his **EPISTEMOLOGY**. He believed that it was impossible to have direct knowledge of God, and thus we could not know what was right and wrong through God's commands, as **DIVINE COMMAND THEORY** would claim.

Equally, we cannot know what is right or wrong though looking at the consequences of an action, as utilitarian theories would claim. This is because all **CONSEQUENCES** belong to the world of experience, what Kant calls the **PHENOMENAL REALM**, and you cannot discover moral value within this realm. For Kant, **MORALITY** is part of the **NOUMENAL REALM**, or the world of reason. Experience, the phenomenal realm, can tell you what to do if you require a certain outcome, but not the things that you should be aiming for - that is the job of **REASON** in the noumenal world.

These two, the **HYPOTHETICAL** and **CATEGORICAL IMPERATIVES**, form the basis of Kant's ethical theory.

There is therefore a moral code which can be known through reason, and it is based on duty. This can be defined as acting morally according to the good regardless of the consequences. You should do something because it is the right thing to do. If something is the right thing to do it is right irrespective of time or place or situation.

Kant says that the only thing that can be said to be good without exception is a **GOOD WILL**. Many other things will be good in certain situations, but only a good will will be good in all. For instance, self-control is good, but can be used by evil people to make their evil deeds more effective.

The idea of a good will is a critical aspect of Kant's moral theory.

THE HYPOTHETICAL IMPERATIVE

Therefore, the hypothetical imperative, as previously discussed is simply what you do if you require a certain outcome (a command to act to achieve a certain result).

For instance, someone might say that you should study under a certain tutor, and read certain books, or use certain tools, if you want to be a good wood engraver. This might be a command because the person giving it wants you to be the best wood engraver, but it is not a moral command.

Equally, someone might require you to wear a certain uniform if you want to go to a specific school. This again is an **IMPERATIVE TO ACT** in a certain way if you want a specific thing. Notice that there is a conditional sense to these commands,"'if you want something, you should do this", rather than simply, "you should do this, no matter what". This would be a categorical imperative.

THE CATEGORICAL IMPERATIVE

This is simply a command to act that is good in itself regardless of consequences. It is the imperative of morality because it can be deduced through reason and universalised.

It can be formulated in three ways:

1. **FORMULA OF THE LAW OF NATURE** - Whereby a maxim can be established as a universal law. Kant says:

   "Act only on that maxim through which you can at the same time will that it should become a universal law".

   An example might be obtaining a loan by making a false promise. If everybody did this, no one would believe such promises. Therefore this maxim contradicts itself. Only maxims which can be universalised without contradiction are valid.

2. **FORMULA OF THE END IN ITSELF** - Whereby people are treated as ends in themselves, not as means to an end. Kant says:

   "Act in such a way that you always treat humanity, whether in your own person or in the person of any other, never simply as a means, but always at the same time as an end".

   This means we should treat people with respect, and not use them to further our own goals. If we don't do this we undermine their status as rational agents.

3. **FORMULA OF THE KINGDOM OF ENDS** - Whereby a society of rationality is established in which people treat each other as ends and not means. Kant says:

   "Every rational being must so act as if he were through his maxims a law-making member in the universal kingdom of ends."

   Kant thinks that one's own reason ought to be able to tell one if something is immoral. For example, obtaining a loan using a false promise cannot be universalised; one's own reason can tell one something that is universally valid, so all other members of a society should be reaching the same conclusions about the maxims.

THE THREE POSTULATES

They are:

1. **FREEDOM**
2. **IMMORTALITY**
3. **GOD**

The postulates are **IMPLICIT ASSUMPTIONS** which according to Kant, every time you act morally you are accepting.

Why?

To act morally you must be free

You must have the ability to freely use your reason to work out the right thing to do; if you are compelled to act in the "right" way your action is not a moral one, because you had no choice in it.

Why should we need immortality then?

Doing the right thing should be crowned with happiness

Kant calls this the **SUMMUM BONUM**.

But it is unusual that doing the right thing makes us happy in this life, therefore, there needs to be a further existence after death in which we can attain the summum bonum.

And of course, if there is an afterlife, there needs to be a God to provide that and to crown us with the summum bonum.

IS NATURAL LAW A HELPFUL METHOD OF MORAL DECISION-MAKING?

Strengths

- **INFLUENTIAL** - It has been highly influential on ethical thought.

- **COHERENT** - It builds a coherent and detailed system, which can deal with many different ethical situations.

- **HARD TO DENY** - Key insights of the theory are hard to deny: it is clear that morality cannot derive from experience alone, or to put it another way, you cannot get an **OUGHT** from an **IS.**

- **STRONGER THAN RELATIVIST THEORIES** - Has none of the weaknesses of relativist theories. There are universal moral absolutes which can be known through reason. This is very clearly the basis of much of the thinking from the Enlightenment, and modern societies and democracies mainly implicitly accept this.

Weaknesses

- **ONLY A THEORY** - It is only a formal theory, which gives no practical guidelines for particular situations. This is very good if you want an account of what morality is, but less helpful if you want to know how to act morally.

- **UNTRIED** - A response to this is that Kant never tries in the Groundwork of the Metaphysic of Morals to lay out practical guidelines - he does this elsewhere.

- **SUSPICIOUS** - Are any actions free from ulterior motives? Can we ever do something purely out of duty?

- **UNEMOTIONAL** - There is little room for emotion or feeling in the system, and yet for many people morality is intimately involved with feeling. For example, I may be moved out of pity to help another. Even Christ at times seemed to be moved in this way before he acted.

- **INFLEXIBLE** - The system seems to be too inflexible, and could give rise to rules which are too rigid or even silly, for instance, the famous example of not lying to the axe-murderer.

NEED MORE HELP ON KANTIAN ETHICS?

Use your phone to scan this QR code

Utilitarianism

Utilitarianism is a **TELEOLOGICAL** ethical theory which employs the concept of utility in a relativist approach. Utility could be defined as seeking the greatest balance of good over evil, or pleasure over pain. Utilitarianism was first propounded by **JEREMY BENTHAM** in 1789.

The **PRINCIPLE OF UTILITY** is simply that the best consequences should be brought about from any action.

It is a **CONSEQUENTIALIST** theory which defines the right action as one that will bring about the greatest good.

A simple slogan for utilitarian theories might be **THE END JUSTIFIES THE MEANS**.

KEYWORDS

- **UTILITY** - Key principle of Utilitarianism - criterion of usefulness of an action
- **CONSEQUENTIALISM** - Moral system in which the results or consequences of an action are key to deciding its value
- **HEDONIC CALCULUS** - System invented by Jeremy Bentham in which pleasure and pain are weighed against each other to decide on whether a course of action should be pursued
- **QUANTITATIVE** - Relating to quantity
- **QUALITATIVE** - Relating to quality
- **HIERARCHY** - System of sacred order, in which the greater quality is placed above that of greater quantity
- **TYRANNY OF THE MAJORITY** - Term to describe the imposition of the wishes of the many over the wishes of the few
- **SELF-EVIDENT** - Inherently obvious, clear from the description
- **NATURALISTIC FALLACY** - Error of reasoning in which an "is" is derived from an "ought" - eg, feeling jealous is only natural, therefore there is nothing wrong with feeling jealous

THE HEDONIC CALCULUS

It is calculating the **BENEFIT** or **HARM** of an act through its consequences. When a utilitarian wants to know what will produce the greatest happiness they need to do a calculation or measurement.

How do you measure happiness? Bentham proposed the **HEDONIC CALCULUS** which quantified pleasure using seven measures:

1. **INTENSITY** - If pleasure lacks intensity its value decreases on the scale

2. **DURATION -** If the pleasure is short-lived its value is lower

3. **CERTAINTY** or **UNCERTAINTY -** How likely is the action to cause pleasure?

4. **PROPINQUITY** - Also means nearness or remoteness

5. **FECUNDITY** - The likelihood of its being followed by other similar sensations

6. **PURITY** - The likelihood of its not being followed by opposite: painful sensations

7. **EXTENT** - The number of people affected by it

ACT UTILITARIANISM

Proposed by **JEREMY BENTHAM**, Act Utilitarianism was the original form of the theory, and is viewed by many as less sophisticated than later versions. Jeremy Bentham was born into a wealthy family in 1748 and died in 1842. His body has been preserved and is in a glass display case in University College London.

ACT UTILITARIANISM is focused on individual situations and particular actions, thus - the act. Bentham was influenced by Locke and Hume, and his empiricist and analytical approach led him to focus on actions which he believed could be given a quantitative value and weighed against the value of other actions to decide on the best course of action.

It is a relative ethical theory; as in all consequentialist theories, the assumption is that what is right will vary from situation to situation. There is also a moral and psychological individualism to the theory - for Bentham the self is the fundamental unit, and there is no real other unit such as society or the church etc. This means that what is pleasurable or painful to the individual is to be given supreme importance in deciding on actions.

This individualism is a result of the emphasis on human reasoning in the Enlightenment. Duncan and Gray say that for Bentham:

"The individual human being is conceived as the source of values and as himself the supreme value." (Duncan, Graeme & Gray, John. "The Left Against Mill, " in New

Essays on John Stuart Mill and Utilitarianism, Eds. Wesley E. Cooper, Kai Nielsen and Steven C. Patten, 1979.)

Bentham's theory is also quantitative - the hedonic calculus reduces happiness to a quantity worked out through an equation. This strikes many as rather odd, and in practice extremely difficult to do.

The theory is based on pleasure, thus hedonistic - Bentham takes it that the principle thing individuals do is to avoid pain and seek pleasure. This view of human nature has been contested by many before and after. For instance, Plato thinks that when humans know what is good for them they will seek that good, even if it doesn't immediately satisfy any hedonic calculus.

Ultimately act utilitarianism follows one principle - the **PRINCIPLE OF UTILITY** - and that must be adhered to. But the principle, that the best consequences should be brought out of any action, is not rich enough to provide sufficient moral guidance.

RULE UTILITARIANISM

Proposed by **JOHN STUART MILL,** rule utilitarianism is a later theory which significantly modified Bentham's earlier work. In broadening and giving a more sophisticated account of happiness, Mill manages to create a moral theory which has some value.

Instead of happiness as pleasure, Mill focuses on happiness in a broader sense. This is quite an obvious move, as the study of happiness by many philosophers throughout the ages has yielded a vast amount of thought as to what happiness is. It was quite simple for Mill to expand the definition of happiness into a hierarchical scheme.

The key thing that Mill does here is to identify and distinguish between **HIGHER PLEASURES** and **LOWER PLEASURES**. Some examples might be: eating a cream cake is a lower pleasure compared to learning to play an instrument; making money is a lower pleasure than using that money to fund philanthropic ventures.

There is also a difference in Mill's principle of utility: Happiness is desirable. Happiness is the only thing desirable as an end in itself – the general happiness of all is desirable. Increasing the happiness of others increases your own. Psychological studies have recently shown this to be true - reducing happiness to seeking pleasure and avoiding pain does not do justice to the complexity of the human search for happiness.

Mill had general rules which were applied universally across societies to promote happiness, thus his theory is not quantitative or relativist like act utilitarianism. It could be said to be qualitative in that it looks at higher and lower pleasures, and judges some as intrinsically more valuable than others.

IS UTILITARIANISM A HELPFUL METHOD OF MORAL DECISION-MAKING?

Strengths

- **JUSTIFIED** - Mill addresses the problem of justifying the principle of utility with some degree of success.

- **HAPPINESS RULES** - He acknowledges that it cannot be proved but points out that happiness is the only thing desirable as an end in itself, and that everything we do is usually done for its sake.

- **GREATEST HAPPINESS PRINCIPLE** - Therefore, as everything we do is either a form of happiness or a means to happiness, the greatest happiness principle can be accepted as a fundamental principle of morality, as it is in line with the ultimate goal to which we direct our lives.

- **ATTRACTIVE SIMPLICITY** - Bentham's system has an attractive simplicity, which (if it worked!) would count towards its usefulness as a moral theory.

Weaknesses

▸ Mill's problems with Bentham's theory

- **UNQUANTIFIABLE** - How is it possible to quantify happiness? Can this be done when faced with an ethical dilemma? Can it be done at all?

- **HARD TO PREDICT** - Problems with the teleological nature of Bentham's theory, it is hard to predict what the consequences will always be of an action.

- **TOO SUBJECTIVE** - What is pleasure? It is too subjective. Some people take pleasure in things that others find painful or repulsive.

- **NO HIERARCHY** - It does not distinguish between different sorts of pleasures. There is no attempt at hierarchy; surely there are nobler and cruder pleasures? Some pleasures are surely little more than animal instincts.

- **TYRANNY OF THE MAJORITY** - Emphasis on greatest good for greatest number leads to a tyranny of the majority. What about the needs of the minority?

▸ Other problems

- **UNJUSTIFIABLE** - How does Bentham justify his principle of utility? He says it does not have to be proved as it is like the first principle of an argument, a self-evident truth.

- **NOT DERIVED FROM HAPPINESS** - Some have noted that Bentham does seem to derive his principle of utility from the observation that the desire for happiness is fundamental to all humans.

- **NATURALISTIC FALLACY** - This would be a case of committing the naturalistic fallacy, of deriving an **IS** from an **OUGHT**.

- **NO MORAL CURRENCY** - Pleasure varies dramatically and it is not clear that all human goals can be expressed in it; for instance, if one person gains deep pleasure from watching another person succeeding at a task, or from helping someone to become well, whilst another person gains pleasure from torturing innocent people or from bingeing on alcohol, then it is difficult to make the notion of pleasure a unit of moral currency.

- **UNWORKABLE** - Mill's richer account of pleasure makes the hedonic calculus unworkable.

NEED MORE HELP ON UTILITARIANISM?

Use your phone to scan this QR code

GOOD ?

BAD?

Euthanasia

The topic of euthanasia raises important moral questions which can be answered in different ways by different moral theories. This section highlights the main issues.

KEYWORDS

- **EUTHANASIA** - "Gentle or easy death" - helping those who are suffering to die

- **SANCTITY OF LIFE** - Christian notion that human life is intrinsically valuable as a creation of God

- **DIGNITY** - Worthy of respect, having intrinsic value as human

- **AUTONOMY** - Controlled by self, rather than another - independence

- **POST-ENLIGHTENMENT** - After the 17th Century philosophical movement which championed reason

- **SLIPPERY SLOPE** - Type of argument in which it is assumed that if certain things are permitted, other more destructive things will follow as a result

WHAT IS EUTHANASIA?

The term could be translated as **GOOD DEATH**; euthanasia is usually seen as killing someone else whose life is not thought worth living.

There is a distinction between active and passive euthanasia:

- **ACTIVE** - Doing something to bring about or hasten the death of the person, such as administering a lethal dose of a drug.

- **PASSIVE** - Causing or hastening death by omitting to do something, or ceasing to provide something that was needed for life to continue. This might be something such as removing feeding tubes.

SANCTITY OF LIFE

Sanctity of life is a notion with roots in the Judaeo-Christian tradition. It is an articulation of an absolute value or intrinsic worth to all human life based on the idea of life as a **GIFT FROM GOD**, the creator of all things, and the particular position of man as the pinnacle of creation on the sixth day, being made in the image and likeness of God.

In **GENESIS**, God creates all things and sees that they are "very good". Created things are dependent on God for their existence. However, their goodness is not simply part of God's substance but is an independent result of their being **GIFTED** their existence by God.

This means that we should value and cherish all life, and particularly human life.

If God is the real owner of all life then we do not have the right to dispose of it as we will - there are limits to what we can do with it.

Therefore, sanctity of life denotes an **UNCONDITIONAL** value to all human life, regardless of age, mental or physical capacity.

In the Encyclical Evangelium vitae, Pope John Paul II draws on the Christian tradition to make the case that suicide is "as morally objectionable as murder". Equally, the Catholic church sees euthanasia - helping someone to commit suicide - as objectionable for the same reasons.

QUALITY OF LIFE

Quality of life arguments are usually set in contrast to sanctity of life arguments, as they emphasise the importance of the capacity of the human person to lead a life in which some level of personal flourishing can occur, or that life should possess certain attributes to be worth living.

Usually, if a very low level of quality of life can be shown, ie. that the person experiences no remittance from constant intense suffering, and is severely incapacitated, then it is argued that the person should not be forced to continue to live against their own wishes.

The concept of quality of life has its origins in secular ideas of human freedom, dignity and autonomy, ideas which clearly are not alien to religious traditions, but which have been developed in different directions by post-enlightenment thinkers.

VOLUNTARY EUTHANASIA

Voluntary euthanasia is done at the request or with the consent of the person wishing to be killed. Voluntary euthanasia and assisted suicide are illegal in Britain, but are legal in the Netherlands and Belgium.

NON-VOLUNTARY EUTHANASIA

Non-voluntary euthanasia is done without the request or consent of the person who is killed. This is because the person is unable to give their consent, due to being in a persistent vegetative state (PVS), or for other reasons such as they are a very severely disabled newborn, or they have advanced Alzheimer's disease.

APPLICATION OF NATURAL LAW TO EUTHANASIA

The Catholic Church has taken a broadly natural law approach to euthanasia. In the thirteenth century Thomas Aquinas took suicide to be wrong because:

- **CONTRARY** - It is contrary to the natural law
- **HARMFUL** - It harms the human community to which the person belongs
- **WRONGFUL TO GOD** - It wrongs God whose gift life is and who alone has power over life and death

The Church has essentially applied this to euthanasia. Euthanasia goes against one of the primary precepts of natural law: to preserve life.

It also goes against the precept to live in an ordered society, as it could be seen as introducing harm and distress into the human community.

For instance, there are very strict rules on the reporting of suicide in the media in the UK, as there is a danger of encouraging impressionable people to do it, which academics argue was the case with the spate of suicides in Bridgend in Wales.

However, the doctrine of double effect, which is a key part of natural law, makes the case that as long as you do not intend to do evil, but to do good, it is acceptable to perform an action that may have the foreseen but unintended side-effect of causing an evil, as long as the evil side-effect is outweighed by the good intention.

This is applicable to euthanasia because large doses of pain-relieving drugs are often given which can have the side-effect of hastening the end of life of a patient – this would be an acceptable approach of natural law.

APPLICATION OF SITUATION ETHICS TO EUTHANASIA

The situationist just has to ask what the most loving thing to do in the situation would be. Clearly, many would argue that it is to help the person to end their suffering. However, some would argue that even if that was the most loving thing to do for the patient, it might not be the most loving thing to do for the loved ones.

For example, **SIMON BINNER** went to a Swiss euthanasia clinic to end his life after suffering from Motor Neurone Disease. In a documentary, his wife said that whilst respecting his decision, she felt he had deprived her and his family of the opportunity to care for him and nurse him through his final days.

A situationist would have to weigh up the different features of each element of this case. It is hard to see how a conclusion could be reached about what the most loving thing to do here is.

EVALUATION OF APPLIED ETHICAL THEORIES TO EUTHANASIA

Some would argue there is no rational basis for placing an **ABSOLUTE VALUE** on life in the way that sanctity of life arguments do:

- **WEAKNESS** - Firstly, from a secular viewpoint, scriptural or religious foundations for notions are seen as weak, because they simply do not have any more authority than a story.

  Therefore, to say that life has value because God created it carries little weight if you don't believe in God. However, some secular atheists do argue that life has an intrinsic value simply as human life.

- **OPENNESS TO DEATH** - Secondly, there are some religious viewpoints which point out that to seek to avoid death at all costs goes against the heart of what many religions preach, which is an openness to death.

In Christian traditions, martyrs have been honoured as those who die at the hand of those who hate the faith. But these people have not sought martyrdom, and therefore there can hardly be a comparison to ending life through euthanasia.

HUME pointed out that if there are limits on what I can do with my life as a loan from God, then they should apply not only to artificially ending my life, but to artificially prolonging my life through medicine etc.

UTILITARIAN approaches are also problematic; as we have seen, it might be hard to weigh the different needs of different people in the situation.

However, **PETER SINGER** argues that, in seeking to satisfy the preferences of all concerned, we can come to a coherent decision about suicide and euthanasia. If someone experiences their life as a terrible burden, to permit euthanasia could come close to satisfying the preferences of the ill person and their loved ones.

CONSEQUENTIALIST arguments can contribute to a **SLIPPERY SLOPE** argument against euthanasia. Examples usually point to the consequences on the old or infirm of legal euthanasia putting pressure on them to end their lives.

NEED MORE HELP ON EUTHANASIA?

Use your phone to scan this QR code

Business Ethics

"Being good is good business"

Anita Roddick

"A business that makes nothing but money is a poor kind of business"

Henry Ford

The ethical responsibility of companies, as well as larger questions about the ethical dimension of economics are discussed in this section.

KEYWORDS

- **CORPORATE SOCIAL RESPONSIBILITY** - A company's initiatives to take responsibility for their effect on environmental and social wellbeing

- **SHAREHOLDER** - Any person that owns at least one share of a company's stock

- **FLOURISHING** - State of personal fulfillment in which one's natural capacities are developed and practiced for the benefit of oneself and others

- **WEALTH** - Riches, monetary or otherwise

- **STAKEHOLDERS** - Anyone with a stake in a company, either internal or external, eg. a customer or employer

- **WHISTLE-BLOWING** - The practice of revealing dubious or unethical practices at a corporation by an employee

- **GLOBALISATION** - Gradual homogenisation of markets in different countries due to increased ease of communication and travel

- **FAIR TRADE** - Ethically based initiative which aims to give local producers a fair wage in a multinational system which often results in injustice and inequality due to maximum profit being sought

- **ENNUI** - State of boredom or listlessness resulting from lack of meaning or significance to life

- **CAPITALISM -** Economic system based on private ownership.

- **CONSUMERISM** - Culture in which everything has a price, ideology which encourages consumption

- **DISTRIBUTISM** - Economic ideology based on the principles of Catholic Social Teaching

- **CAPITAL** - Any non-financial asset that is used in production of goods or services

- **EQUITABLE** - Fair and equal

- **SUBSIDIARITY** - An organising principle that matters ought to be handled by the smallest, lowest or least centralised competent authority

- **SOLIDARITY** - A firm and persevering determination to devote oneself to the common good

CORPORATE SOCIAL RESPONSIBILITY

Businesses have a **DUTY** and a **RESPONSIBILITY** to consider the effects of their activities on communities and the environment. When a company monitors its activities and ensures that it complies with the law as well as ethical norms, this is called **CORPORATE SOCIAL RESPONSIBILITY** (CSR).

The fundamental aim of a business could be framed in terms of making a profit. If this key aim of shareholders is allowed to override all other considerations then it becomes a matter of **ETHICAL CONCERN**.

A broader formulation of the aim of a business could be to generate wealth. Wealth is something that can be considered in purely monetary terms, but also in terms of human flourishing. If a business succeeds at generating these different forms of wealth it could be seen as an ethically responsible business.

This approach is often phrased as **GOOD ETHICS IS GOOD BUSINESS**; below are some examples of the interrelationship between these areas:

- **WORKERS** - For instance, a business might look after its workers and train them, provide opportunities for professional development and so on; this is good business sense because happy workers are productive workers.

- **ENVIRONMENT** - A company may get involved in local environmental schemes, such as tree-planting etc; this would not only offset any negative impact their **CARBON FOOTPRINT** makes, but also provide opportunities for a positive profile in the local area, and thus encourage more people to do business with them.

However, some would disagree with the broad formulation of the aim of a business to generate wealth not only in monetary terms.

For example, **MILTON FRIEDMAN** (1912-2006) an American economist, said that a business's social responsibility lies purely in increasing its profits, and that as long as it stays within the rules of the game, it should be able to freely engage in competition with a view to doing simply this.

INTERNAL & EXTERNAL STAKEHOLDERS

The idea of the corporate social responsibility of a business means that a business is obliged to consider different stakeholders. There are two types:

- **INTERNAL STAKEHOLDERS** - These are owners, managers, workers and suppliers, who respectively, are interested in; making a profit, earning a salary, keeping their jobs and earning high wages, and continuing to supply businesses with their products.

- **EXTERNAL STAKEHOLDERS** - These are customers, the local community and the local environment; these different groups have an interest in being able to buy good quality products at reasonable prices, having a reliable employer to keep local people in work, and wanting a business to impact positively on their environment, without air or noise pollution.

What kind of responsibility companies have to internal and external stakeholders will be the job of ethical theories to decide.

WHISTLE-BLOWING

The relationship between employer and employee is complex. This relationship is defined in law by a contract. There are also ethical considerations to be made in certain circumstances. For instance if an employee witnesses or learns of wrongdoing on the part of the employer, should they disclose this to others or the public? This is called **WHISTLE-BLOWING**.

Whistle-blowing raises questions of confidentiality and loyalty. How does an employee decide what it is in the public interest to know about the company?

Most would agree that it is easier to argue for whistle-blowing if there are issues of safety or financial misdemeanours at stake. With the advent of the internet it is now very easy for individuals to disseminate information about companies widely and there are several websites that exist to protect whistle-blowers.

GLOBALISATION

Globalisation refers to the fact that around the world economies, industries, markets, cultures and policy-making are becoming increasingly **MORE INTEGRATED**. Essentially, the differences between one economy and another are reduced, so that trade all over the world becomes increasingly similar.

Globalisation has increased in recent times for various reasons such as:

- **TRANSPORT** - Has become speedier and less costly

- **TECHNOLOGICAL CHANGE** - The internet and global communication have meant faster exchange of information

- **EMERGING MARKETS** - Developing countries provide new opportunities

- **FREE TRADE** - The removal of trade barriers, for instance, the EU

Some ethical issues related to globalisation are:

- **CHEAP LABOUR** - Companies are now freer to base themselves in countries where labour is cheap to reduce manufacturing costs. This can lead to **SWEAT SHOPS** and child workers.

- **FAIR TRADE** - Trade between countries can be unfair, with rich countries having very strong trade barriers.

- **CULTURAL EROSION** - As one-world markets emerge, the danger is that consumer culture begins to replace individual and cultural identities, with the loss of ancient traditions and the homogenisation of ways of living.

KANTIAN APPROACHES TO BUSINESS ETHICS

MILTON FRIEDMAN's standpoint, that a business's only responsibility is to its shareholders, would be disputed by Kant, who believed that people should not be used as a means to an end. If the workers are simply used as a means to make a profit, this goes against one of the basic tenets of Kantian ethics. Kantian ethics considers all stakeholders as worthy of consideration, and the owner of the business should act as a law-making member of a **KINGDOM OF ENDS**.

In terms of whistle-blowing, Kantian ethics considers what it is your duty to do. Your duty overrides any loyalty you might feel towards the company. If the safety of workers is at stake, you have a duty to protect them by blowing the whistle, regardless of whether it will cause you to lose your job.

UTILITARIAN APPROACHES TO BUSINESS ETHICS

In seeking to promote the **GREATEST GOOD** of the **GREATEST NUMBER**, utilitarianism would seem to be favourable to the workers, who outnumber the managers in business. Utilitarianism would stress the importance of workers' rights, and indeed, most forms of socialism and communism would have a utilitarian background.

However, utilitarian arguments might promote questionable business practices, as long as those practices favoured the greatest good of the greatest number.

For instance, if a local area was to be blighted by a factory, but many people would gain from the job opportunities it brought to the area, then essentially the suffering of those in the neighbourhood of the factory would be ignored. This is called the **TYRANNY OF THE MAJORITY**.

CAN HUMAN BEINGS FLOURISH IN THE CONTEXT OF CAPITALISM AND CONSUMERISM?

Capitalism relies on a **COMPETITIVE INDIVIDUALISM** which can foster great social inequalities. In the context of rampant consumerism, demand for cheap products will mean poor working conditions for many.

Equally, the **CONSUMERISM** of modern developed societies can foster a selfishness and ennui, a kind of spiritual void, which people attempt to fill with more material goods. In such a context it becomes difficult to experience the world as gift, to be thankful with little, and to understand one's self as a being created for a deeper purpose than material acquisition.

As previously mentioned, wealth can be viewed in ways other than the purely monetary kind. The right kind of wealth-creation might actually enable human flourishing. What might that look like?

A system devised in the early twentieth century by **G K CHESTERTON**, **HILAIRE BELLOC** and others called **DISTRIBUTISM**, aimed at promoting an economic vision in which human flourishing is central. Some of its key ideas are:

- **LEVEL THE FIELD** - As long as capital is in the hands of a few massive corporations, inequalities and injustices will continue; far more people could be given incentives to go into business, and this would create more equitable conditions.

- **THE INVISIBLE HAND OF THE MARKET** - Should not be allowed to run things; state control would have to be stronger and more prevalent to stop irresponsible speculation, and make sure businesses were run ethically.

- **THE CATHOLIC CHURCH** - Has promoted in many of its encyclicals a vision very similar to this; for instance, in Rerum Novarum, Pope Leo XIII laid out fundamental principles for the relationship between labour and capital, including: the dignity of the human person, the common good, subsidiarity, participation, solidarity, the right of private property and the universal destination of goods. These principles form the backbone of **CATHOLIC SOCIAL TEACHING**.

NEED MORE HELP ON BUSINESS ETHICS?

Use your phone to scan this QR code

Developments in Christian Thought

(H173/Component 03)

Insight

Foundations

Living

Introducing Developments in Christian Thought

The history of Christian thought and its evolution is a complex 2000 year-long process. The specification breaks this down into 3 basic areas: insight, foundations and morality. The first section explores human nature as it relates to the purpose of life, the self and the afterlife. The theology of St.Augustine on human nature, sin and grace is examined and evaluated in the light of modern critiques. The concepts of heaven, hell and purgatory are explored, as well as the different approaches to election.

The section on knowledge of God examines the distinction between natural and revealed knowledge with an emphasis on Calvin's thought and the legacy of the distinction in the Barth-Brunner debate. Essentially, this is a debate about the limits of knowledge of God and whether our ability to know Him is radically corrupted by Original Sin.

Different understandings of the person of Christ are then examined; namely the idea of Jesus as liberator, son of God, or teacher of wisdom. This debate leads into modern understandings of Jesus in Black and Liberation Theology. One interesting question is whether modern scholarship is able to defend interpretations of the person of Jesus based on liberal or conservative outlooks.

The final section of the book looks at Christian ethics through the lens of principles and action. This leads into questions as to the authority of the Bible, whether Christian ethical principles can be defended on the basis of scripture alone, and whether Christian ethics can be reduced to the command to love God and neighbour. The guide ends as it began, with a study of an influential Christian figure, that of Dietrich Bonhoeffer, whose life and actions should be seen in the context of his theology.

SAINT AUGUSTINE

St Augustine

INTRODUCTION

The fundamental insights of theology in this module relate to what is often called the human condition. This refers to a large range of ideas, but some of the key elements include such questions as why we find ourselves unable to persist in virtue without falling prey to disordered appetites, how life can have meaning in the face of death, what place suffering and evil might have, if any, in God's plan, and whether it is possible to transcend the **FALLEN** condition we find ourselves in.

The classical Christian answers to all these questions can all be found in the work of **ST. AUGUSTINE**, and this theologian is still profoundly important to the ongoing debates in this area.

KEYWORDS

- **PARADISE** - State of original perfection or final dwelling of the soul with God

- **THE FALL** - Event which was brought about by an original act of disobedience of God's command - resulting in loss of grace and stain of original sin on humanity

- **ORIGINAL PERFECTION** - State of humanity before the Fall in which humans possessed God's grace, and no evil or imperfection had entered the world

- **ORIGINAL SIN** - Mark or stain possessed by all humans following the original disobedience of Adam and Eve, which results in a disordered will and the presence of cupiditas in human nature

- **BEFORE THE FALL (PRE-FALL)** - State of humankind in paradise before the original disobedience of Adam and Eve

- **AFTER THE FALL (POST-FALL)** - State of humankind after the original disobedience of Adam and Eve in which they are banished from paradise

- **CARITAS** - The pre-Fall state of the will in which it chooses generously and is motivated by love of God and others

- **CUPIDITAS** - The post-Fall state of the will in which it chooses selfishly and is motivated by lust and other selfish desires

- **CONCUPISCENCE** - Lack of mastery over the passions resulting from the loss of God's grace after the Fall

- **GRACE** - Supernatural gift of God to intellectual creatures for their eternal salvation

- **SANCTIFYING GRACE** - Supernatural infusion of God in the soul, by which a person participates in the divine life

- **HABITUAL GRACE** - See sanctifying grace

- **PRIVATION** - A lack of something that should be present, eg, a broken chair might have a privation of the strength in the wood

- **EXISTENTIALISM** - 20th century school of philosophy in which existence is thought to precede essence

- **BAD FAITH** - Sartre's term for the inauthentic life, lived according to another's rules and not one's own

- **ONTOLOGICAL** - To do with existence or being

- **RENUNCIATION** - Process of giving up things to which one is attached

AUGUSTINE'S TEACHING ON HUMAN NATURE

What is human nature?

Is there something that human beings are like? Do we as a species possess universal traits, flaws or aptitudes which prescribe the limits within which we must live? For instance, are we irredeemably aggressive and selfish, or do we all have the capacity for tolerance and altruism? We could single out some attributes that many thinkers have thought we all possess:

- **DESIRE TO BE HAPPY** - Something that everyone seeks is happiness

- **GENDERED** - Is our worldview different if seen through male/female eyes?

- **LIMITED BY DEATH** - No matter what plans we have we are aware that death can take them away

- **SELFISHNESS/SINFULNESS** - We may desire to be good, but we all experience sinful/selfish impulses

St. Augustine (354-430 AD) put these characteristics into a Christian explanatory framework, and used the book of Genesis to understand how human nature came to be as it is.

Human Relationships pre- & post-Fall

Genesis 3 uses the story of Adam and Eve in the garden of Eden to narrate how humanity went from a **STATE OF ORIGINAL PERFECTION** to a **FALLEN DISORDERED STATE** of sin characterised by selfish desires and lust.

Some of the key points are:

- **UNIQUE STATUS** - God created humans in his "image and likeness", which implies a unique status in creation
- **HARMONIOUS RELATIONSHIP OF FRIENDSHIP** - No animal was suitable as a companion for Adam, so God created Eve from Adam - Adam and Eve lived in a harmonious relationship of friendship
- **STATE OF INNOCENCE** - They also lived in a harmonious relationship with God and the natural world - a state of innocence
- **OBEDIENCE TO GOD** - This harmony is expressed in their obedience to God, and in their responsibility to the natural world (eg. naming the animals)
- **COOPERATION** - Augustine interprets this harmony internally as well - human will, desires and reason were in total cooperation with each other
- **MOTIVATION** - Before the fall, the free will chooses generously - it is motivated by love of God and our fellow beings.
- **CARITAS** - Augustine calls this motivation caritas, or selfless love
- **BEFORE THE FALL** - Before the fall the relationship of Adam and Eve as friends occurs even in sexual reproduction which takes place without lust
- **AFTER THE FALL** - We are diminished and our will chooses selfishly
- **CUPIDITAS** - Augustine calls the selfishly motivated will cupiditas
- **SEX IS SECONDARY** - Friendship marked the marriage of Adam and Eve according to Augustine - but sex is secondary to friendship
- **ORIGINAL SENSE** - After the Fall, friendship still expresses some of its original sense of caritas as love of God, but can only be truly found by those who love Christ first

Original Sin and its Effects on the Will and Human Societies

The will, as we have seen, was profoundly marked by **THE FALL**. It is divided and therefore weak. Augustine sees the rebellious state of the will as a direct result of Adam's sin of disobedience.

Adam's **SIN OF DISOBEDIENCE** was the cause of the state in which we find ourselves - that of Original Sin. This is a hereditary stain with which we are born as a result of Adam's sin.

Romans 5:12 is a key text:

> *"It was through one man that guilt came into the world; and, since death came owing to guilt, death was handed on to all mankind by one man."*

ORIGINAL SIN only deprives man of those Divine gifts to which his nature had no right; humans have not lost the possession of their natural faculties such as reason. Some of the effects of Original Sin are:

- **CONCUPISCENCE** - This is the privation of the complete mastery over the passions which was a **DIVINE GIFT**. In other words man is no longer able to control his appetites, including his libido (sexual desire). This does not mean that the body is evil - the body is created good (see Genesis), but the will is divided and weak, and this means that the appetites can dominate - therefore the body can be overrun by gluttony, love of money and power, and sexual desire.

- **DEATH OF THE BODY** - Romans is clear that this is one of the results of Original Sin.

- **PRIVATION OF SANCTIFYING GRACE** - Death of the soul. Not only does the body dies as a result of Original Sin, but humans are also deprived of grace - this is holiness, and holiness is union with God. Grace is not any particular good act, but a permanent tendency towards God as we shall see. Without grace the soul cannot live, as vices grow stronger and choke its life.

- **PRIVATION OF THE VISION OF GOD** - Augustine argues that our true end in the next life is the beatific vision - seeing God. Without the effect of grace, it is impossible to see God, as the soul's vision is distorted by the appetites. The beatitude says:

"Blessed are the pure in heart, for they shall see God"

Matt 5

God's Grace

GRACE is a supernatural gift of God to intellectual creatures (humans and angels) for their eternal salvation. It is a generous and loving act of God, which is completely undeserved by humans. Christ's saving action of death on the cross is considered the supreme example. Augustine said that the entire drama of Christianity could be expressed in the intervention of two men, the one to ruin us, the other to save us.

God gave his son Jesus Christ and the guilt of the Original Sin is removed - humanity is redeemed. There would be no possibility of redemption without this **GRACE OF GOD**.

Because Augustine experienced the strong and persistent effect of sinful desires in his life - his memories of past pleasures - he was able to ask St. Paul:

"Who will deliver me from this body of death?"

Romans 7:24

The only possible answer is God - no mere human effort can achieve this on its own. God takes a step towards humankind in the person of Jesus Christ, and our sinful natures are capable of redemption.

EVALUATION OF AUGUSTINE'S TEACHING ON HUMAN NATURE

Is Talk of an Historical Fall and Original Sin Mistaken?

Augustine is clear that the Fall is considered as an actual historical event, and that because we were all present in Adam then we are all liable for the consequences of the Fall. There are some fairly strong challenges to this position.

- **COLIN GUNTON** - Argued for a non-literal reading - Genesis understood as our potential in the light of the eschaton (last judgement)

- **DAWKINS CONSIDERS IT ABSURD** - Corruption of all humans rests on two individuals. Evolution also prevents a historical fall from being a reality - humans emerged from less sophisticated animals and so couldn't have rebelled with a primitive consciousness.

- **ORIGINAL SIN - EXISTENTIALISTS** - Sartre considers there is no fixed human nature as this would compromise our freedom. All we have to do is to decide whether to live authentically - anything else is BAD FAITH . There is thus no Original Sin. In fact, the only sin is to live inauthentically.

- **THE CATHOLIC CHURCH FOLLOWS AUGUSTINE** - The CCC states:

    "The account of the fall in Genesis 3 uses figurative language, but affirms a primeval event, a deed that took place at the beginning of the history of man. Revelation gives us the certainty of faith that the whole of human history is marked by the original fault freely committed by our first parents."

- **THE REALITY OF EVIL** - Suffering in the world which has its origin in human action or lack of action is something that theists need to explain. Augustine's account of the Fall does require a certain view of human history that is fairly **ALTERNATIVE**

Does Sin Mean that Humans Can Never Be Good?

Augustine's account of sin as an **ONTOLOGICAL** mark - a privation in our very being - means that no matter how hard we try we cannot by our own efforts free ourselves from this **BODY OF DEATH** - it is only through grace that we are saved.

However, through constant effort (though not solely effort) we can establish **HABITUAL GRACE** in our souls. It is a state in which we possess virtues that God gives us by having established a permanent habit of turning towards God.

Augustine insists on a **GRACE OF PERSEVERANCE**, one with a habitual grace can, with correct action, merit more habitual grace:

"Charity merits increase, and being increased merits to be perfected".

This is tempered by the fact that this healing which is brought about by grace is never complete in this life. The person with habitual grace is still assailed by internal and external temptations.

So it is clearly possible for people to be good in Augustine's scheme; they are just profoundly limited by the weakness and division of the will bequeathed by Original Sin. Without the necessary **RENUNCIATION** needed in order to follow Christ, it will be very difficult for people to be good.

Is Augustine's View of Human Nature Pessimistic or Optimistic?

There is an obvious response to this question, in that Augustine is probably best described as a realist when it comes to human nature! He doesn't deny that we can do good with God's help, but he also makes it clear that we are in a weakened state with regard to our will.

There are many post-Enlightenment views of human nature which appear far too optimistic about what human nature is capable of. The liberal **GOSPEL OF PROGRESS** assumes that the more we divest ourselves from superstitious and primitive beliefs, the more we will free ourselves from violence and conflict, which has been shown to be dangerously naive.

For instance, **JOSEPH RATZINGER, POPE EMERITUS BENEDICT XVI** says in **SPE SALVI**:

> *"Theodor W. Adorno formulated the problem of faith in progress quite drastically: he said that progress, seen accurately is progress from the sling to the atom bomb ...The ambiguity of progress becomes evident. Without doubt, it offers new possibilities for good, but it also opens up appalling possibilities for evil."*

The more we come to terms with the radical privation in our being, the closer we will come to being realistic about what we are capable of as humans, says Augustine. This seems a prudent viewpoint.

Is there a Distinctive Human Nature?

We have already seen the existentialist claim that there is no fixed human nature. How did they arrive at this conclusion? Here is a brief overview:

- **EXISTENCE PRECEDES ESSENCE** - This overturns the traditional view that essence precedes existence, that we have a given nature which determines what our lives will be like

- **WE HAVE NO PREDETERMINED NATURE** - We are what we do

- **WE ARE RADICALLY FREE** - To act independently

- **WE CREATE OUR HUMAN NATURE** - Our values are created through the choices we make

This is not necessarily a strictly deductive argument, more a complete turning on its head of the traditional notion of essence. It is worth noting that the idea of essence by the twentieth century had suffered some major damage. Sartre is merely following these leads to their logical conclusions.

If the existentialists are right, it is possible that we could free ourselves by accepting the thrownness, anxiety and despair which comes with having no external value or purpose - this would also of course mean rejecting any traditional notion of morality. As Dostoevsky has one of his characters, Ivan Karamazov, say:

"If God is dead, then everything is permitted".

It is more in keeping with the insights of psychologists and even many philosophers, that there is, in fact, a human nature, and that it may be elusive, but it lies at the basis of both human creativity and aggression.

NEED MORE HELP ON ST AUGUSTINE?

Use your phone to scan this QR code

Death and the Afterlife

From **AQUINAS** to **HICK**, key questions relating to death and the afterlife have been debated in theology. But such fundamental questions as what relation moral actions have to the afterlife, and what happens when we die, have also inspired and informed great works of literature and poetry, such as Dante's Commedia. Until recent times the notion of "extra ecclesia nullas salus" (no salvation outside the Church) guided Catholic theology in the area of salvation. However, the modern Catholic church has reinterpreted this for the religiously pluralistic times in which we live.

KEYWORDS

- **INFERNO** - Work by Dante - Italian word for Hell

- **LIMBO** - Intermediate place in afterlife where the pious unbaptised live

- **HELL** - Place of suffering and punishment to which Christians believe unrepentant sinners are sent by God

- **LUST** - Desire, usually of a sexual nature

- **PURGATORY** - Place of cleansing of one's soul in the afterlife, in preparation for its meeting with God in heaven

- **DAMNATION** - State of being placed outside of salvation in hell

- **HEAVEN** - State of blissful abiding with God in afterlife as reward for actions in this life

- **GLUTTONY** - Sinful ingestion of large amounts of food - greed

- **MEANNESS** - Being ungenerous with any riches that one might have

- **WRATH** - Misplaced anger

- **HERESY** - Preaching of untrue teachings

- **VIOLENCE** - Physical aggression

- **FRAUD** - Deception practiced for personal gain

- **TREACHERY** - Betrayal

- **COMMUNION OF SAINTS** - The Catholic belief that the Church consists not just of the living, but also those who have died and are in heaven, who can intercede for those on earth with God

- **BEATIFIC VISION** - The blissful union of the soul with God in heaven

- **ESCHATOLOGY/ESCHATOLOGICAL** - To do with the last things, or the end times

- **RESURRECTION** - Belief in physical survival after death, at a point in the future

- **ELECTION** - Being chosen by God for salvation

- **PREDESTINATION** - Belief that God has chosen some people for salvation and others for damnation

CHRISTIAN TEACHING ON HEAVEN, HELL AND PURGATORY

Hell

The medieval view of hell is best exemplified in **DANTE ALIGHIERI'S** work **THE DIVINE COMEDY**. This is the view of hell that has stayed in the popular imagination. In his **INFERNO**, Dante imagines hell as having nine circles, each one deeper below the earth, and each one home to a class of sinner worse than the previous one.

Obviously the Inferno is an allegorical work, but its power lies in its use of Christian symbolism and dogma coupled with profound insight into human nature.

There is a sign at the entrance to hell which says **ABANDON HOPE ALL YE WHO ENTER HERE**. Hell is seen throughout most of Christian thought as a place of eternal punishment - the sinner is never freed, and the loss of hope is almost worse than the actual punishments. However, as we shall see, this view did not remain unchallenged, especially in the twentieth century.

The first circle is called **LIMBO**, and it is a place for the unbaptised who have lived virtuous lives, but who died without access to the revelation of Jesus Christ (either by having the misfortune to live before he came to earth, or living somewhere where the Gospel has never been heard). It is here that Christ visited when he **DESCENDED INTO HELL** between his death and resurrection.

The circles are allocated to certain sins, each progressively more serious:

- **LUST**

- **GLUTTONY**

- **MEANNESS**

- **WRATH**

- **HERESY**

- **VIOLENCE**

- **FRAUD**

- **TREACHERY**

Dante cleverly shows how one sin leads to another, how **PAOLO** and **FRANCESCA** in the circle of the lustful have convinced themselves of the rightness of their illicit union, and how when lust is excused it leads to a sense of entitlement which begets greed, and once greed has satiated itself it isn't satisfied with mere acquisition, but wants to keep everything for itself (the miserly). It is easy to see then how this meanness and lack of generosity leads to anger at others and so on.

What Dante is doing here is exemplifying the doctrine of the insubstantiality of evil - evil as a privation - at the same time as showing how the weak and divided will can be pulled in different directions by the appetites until there is no going back. Because evil is a lack of being, it can never satisfy the human soul, rather it eats away at the virtues of the soul, creating a void of misery which can never be filled.

To a large extent the debt is to **THOMAS AQUINAS**, but through him we can see Augustine as well.

The view of hell as a place of eternal hellfire and divine vengeance or punishment is based in large part on certain passages in scripture. Christ spoke many times of hell in this way, for example, in the parable of the Rich Man and Lazarus, the parable of the Sheep and the Goats, and other places. Always, Christ links the punishment to a lack of charity to others, so that the punishment almost seems self-inflicted:

> *"By the measure with which you measure you will be measured"*

The idea of hell as a place of eternal punishment has been criticised:

- **CONTRADICTORY** - It seems to contradict the view that God will have a final victory over evil.

- **GOD IS LOVE** - It also seems to contradict the view that God is Love. If someone sins and is unrepentant and goes to hell, then would a loving, forgiving God condemn them to eternal torture for a finite amount of sin? However, some would argue it is equally contradictory not to have hell because it would make a mockery of faith in God. If everyone is saved in the end no matter what they do then why bother being good or loving God at all? The view that afterlife punishment is not eternal is known variously as apokatastasis or universalism, and these will be discussed below under "election".

- **LOSS OF BELIEF** - For some, the modern age is characterised by a loss of belief or interest in hell, even on the part of committed Christians, and a focus on love and mercy instead. Some consider that any focus on God's punishment or judgement will drive people away from the faith, as the supreme ideal of modern secular worldviews is tolerance, which means non-judgemental attitudes coupled with a sense of relativism about morality. Any appeal to an absolute morality, or talk of sin, is seen to be 'backward' and 'hate-filled'. This is ironic, as the Church has always considered that one of the most charitable things you can do for another is to gently but firmly correct them when they go astray. Certainly, Christians would view God as desiring us to be guided towards acting rightly, just as a loving parent would do for their child.

It could be seen then, that Christian attempts to downplay hell and judgement would actually backfire in two senses:

- **WHY BOTHER?** - People may think "it's ok I don't have to worry about my sins, God will forgive me no matter what I do", therefore, why bother practising a faith?

- **ROAD TO DAMNATION** - As a pastoral attitude it fails to have a proper care of souls, and sends many down a road to damnation.

Purgatory

Views on purgatory are one of the things that separate Catholics from Protestants. Catholics believe that those who have died in a state of grace are given an opportunity to cleanse themselves of the guilt of their sins before entering heaven. Purgatory is thus an intermediate place of cleansing or purgation.

The notion of purgatory appears to have originated in the practice of praying for the dead in the early Church. For instance, **CLEMENT OF ALEXANDRIA** taught of a purification through fire for those who died without being able to perform works of penance.

Scriptural basis for purgatory include **MACCABEES 12:39-46**, which speaks of penance that can be done for those who have died so that they can be freed from their sin.

The Catholic Church has developed this teaching in the dogma of the **COMMUNION OF SAINTS** and the idea of the holy souls, in which the Church is considered not only to be on earth, but also in eternity, and that each member can have an effect on others through prayer.

> *"From the beginning the Church has honored the memory of the dead and offered prayers in suffrage for them, above all the Eucharistic sacrifice, so that, thus purified, they may attain the beatific vision of God. The Church also commends almsgiving, indulgences, and works of penance undertaken on behalf of the dead."*

CCC 1032

The notion of **PURIFYING FIRE** mentioned earlier was developed in later theology. This was a fire that would have the effect of purging the dross of guilt, and was different from the punishing fire of hell.

CATHERINE OF GENOA, for instance, says that the fires of hell and those of purgatory differ only in the presence of guilt in that of hell, which makes it agonising, whereas the fires of purgatory, because of the anticipation of the beatific vision, are undergone with hope and thus deprived of the agony.

There are some problems with the idea of purgatory:

- **SCRIPTURAL BACKING IS WEAK** - Maccabees is the only place there is a direct reference, and Maccabees is non-canonical to Protestants

- **PROTESTANT** - View of justification by faith makes purgatory superfluous

- **GET-OUT CLAUSE** - How serious would your sin have to be for you not to go to purgatory? If God is all-loving could he not send even unrepentant sinners to purgatory until they learn to love him freely?

- **DOES EVERYONE GO THROUGH PURGATORY?** - This relates to the previous point in that sinners could surely be processed through purgatory for longer rather than going to hell

- **OUTSIDE OF TIME AND SPACE** - If the afterlife happens outside of time and space (God is eternal), then how could duration exist within it - in other words, how could time pass in purgatory? Some have thought that duration will be measured by intensity of the pains of purgatory.

Heaven

Heaven, in the definition of ALISTER MCGRATH, is:

> "the ESCHATOLOGICAL REALISATION of the presence and power of God, and the final elimination of evil'.

In the Catholic tradition it is known as the **BEATIFIC VISION**, the sight of God, an endless mutual loving gaze. Dante is again a source of exemplification - in his **PARADISO** he talks of the love that moves the sun and other stars - the source of all being.

In the New Testament the communal nature of heaven is often emphasised - it is seen variously as a banquet, wedding feast, or the New Jerusalem (Revelation 21). Here, the non-individualistic, mutual sharing of heaven is seen, a reflection of the life of God as Trinity- the relational nature of God as love, which needs lover, beloved and the love between them.

There are two distinct strands of thinking about the afterlife in the Christian tradition which owe something to the influence of Greek philosophy as well as scripture:

- **RESURRECTION** - Here, the emphasis is on the physical re-integration of the body and the soul performed by God on Judgement Day. The **BOOK OF REVELATION** mentions a new heaven and a new earth - the whole of creation is transformed, not destroyed. There is here no treatment of matter as evil, no wish to escape the world, but rather all the goodness of creation is taken up and given its fullest expression which was taken from it by the Fall. This includes human nature

- **DISEMBODIED EXISTENCE** - There is a **PLATONIC INFLUENCE** in Christianity which has been influential and it has led some theologians to stress the non-material aspect of the afterlife. This is the classic view of heaven, of angels floating on clouds which, it has to be said, has had more influence in some protestant traditions than in the Catholic Church

Some of the philosophical issues surrounding the **IDEA OF HEAVEN** are:

- **PERFECTION** - Is the whole of creation transformed and perfected? If so, will you see your pet in heaven? What about worms and flies? Does everything have a place there?

- **WHERE IS HELL?** -   If the whole of creation is transformed, then where is hell? Is hell not eternal? Or is there a place outside of creation reserved for the sinners?

ELECTION

Election is the term for state of being saved from damnation by God. Augustine puts it that the saving action of God is freely given (gratis) as grace to some. Others will not receive it. This means that the elect are those who, through grace, are saved.

It is very important to realise that for Augustine, grace is not a reward, we can do nothing to merit it. God must be free to give or withhold it. Therefore, some will not receive it - by not receiving it they are not elected to salvation, and as many critics pointed out, this means that some are effectively condemned to damnation or at least not to redemption.

The Catholic Church has modified this view, not least because it has some very severe consequences for the nature of God. We shall see below some different viewpoints about who is saved.

Final Judgement & "The Sheep and the Goats"

In the parable of the Sheep and the Goats (Matt 25), Jesus links afterlife reward and punishment with earthly behaviour towards others, and ultimately, to God. Some key points are:

- **FINAL JUDGEMENT** - There will be a final judgement in which the son of man comes to separate the saved from the damned.

- **PAST LIFE** - The judgement about whether one is saved or damned will come down to what we did or did not do for others in our lives.

- **SIX ACTIONS** - There are six actions mentioned: feed the hungry, give drink to the thirsty, give shelter to the homeless, give clothes to the naked, look after the sick, visit those in prison.

- **LOVE THY NEIGHBOUR** - Love of neighbour in fulfilling these charitable actions is revealed to be exactly the same thing as love of God.

- **PIETY IS NOT ENOUGH** - Piety alone, with a lack of kindness to others, will not be enough to save us.

Having looked at the key points of the parable, we shall go over the three main standpoints regarding salvation.

Limited Election

Also called particular redemption, this is the belief that only a few Christians will be saved. It is based in the **REFORMED DOCTRINE OF PREDESTINATION**. If Jesus died to save all of us then there is a problem: some will not be saved. That means that Christ's sacrifice was ineffective for some. However, if Christ died only to save the elect, that means that His sacrifice was effective.

The **FEWNESS OF THE SAVED** seems to have been referred to in the Gospels. Jesus urges his disciples to "strive to enter in at the narrow gate … for many there are who will seek to enter and not be able to". This seems clear enough - even many who think they are heaven-bound because they were Christians will not enter heaven, if they do not do what Christ asks.

Unlimited Election

Unlimited election contrasts with limited election in that it claims that all who believe will be saved. It was an influential and popular view; Aquinas, for instance, stated that an act of faith was necessary for salvation.

In this view, whilst God wishes that all people be saved, it does not mean that he wishes that **EVERY PERSON BE SAVED**, but that all kinds of people should be saved.

This view has been modified to include as believers those who do not have any formal Christian profession of faith, but who by their commitment to goodness and truth are **ANONYMOUS CHRISTIANS**, for example, **C S LEWIS** and **KARL RAHNER**.

Universalism

This means that all will be saved, whether or not they have responded to God's call in Christ. It has very old roots (as the **DOCTRINE OF APOCATASTASIS**). For instance, **ORIGEN** argued that as God could not finally allow the devil to have the souls of the damned in hell forever (because this would be to admit a kind of dualism, equality of good and evil powers, into Christian belief), then God must finally empty hell and save all the damned, human and angel.

In the modern era the philosopher **JOHN HICK** has supported this view. He claims that an all-loving and just God cannot coherently condemn anyone to eternal punishment for finite sins. That would make God a monstrous torturer.

Others point out that universalism makes a mockery of good, moral behaviour in this life, as no matter how evil someone is, they go to heaven. This seems completely unjust, even if they go to heaven after a period of punishment.

> ▶ **DISCUSSION** - *Is heaven the transformation and perfection of the whole of creation?*
>
> ■ **YES** - The book of Revelation talks of 'a new heaven and a new earth'. In 'All things Made New' Stratford Caldecott explores the theological and scriptural backing for the idea. It is a far cry from the "beam-me-up-Scotty" ideas of rapture that some evangelical churches have about last judgement and heaven. To some extent this attitude is the legacy of a Platonic and world-denying influence in Christianity, which actually tends to gnosticism. Far truer to Christianity is the idea of bodily resurrection and the renewal of all creation.
>
> ■ **NO** - Heaven is outside of time and space and is thus an entirely different state of being from life in this world. Any talk of a "new earth" is merely analogical and an attempt to describe the indescribable. If the whole of creation is to be redeemed, then we have to logically fit all creatures into that scheme - what will a "redeemed worm" or mosquito do? Heaven will be an entirely spiritual existence, with no need for physical existence of any sort.

NEED MORE HELP ON DEATH & THE AFTERLIFE?

Use your phone to scan this QR code

Knowledge of God's Existence

The question of the effect the Fall has had on our knowledge of God is at the heart of this module. The modern philosopher Alvin Plantinga argues that the fact that some have religious experiences whilst others never have them, might be attributable to some differences in the functioning of the "religious sense", which could have been damaged by sin to a different degree in different people. This relies on a Calvinist approach to knowledge of God.

KEYWORDS

- **NATURAL THEOLOGY** - Knowledge of God can be found in the natural world

- **REVEALED THEOLOGY** - Knowledge of God comes only through his revelation to us, for example, in scripture

- **INNATE** - An inborn talent or ability

- **SENSUS DIVINITATIS** - Natural ability to know God

- **SEMEN RELIGIONIS** - Seed of faith

- **SERVILE** - Showing a willingness to serve

- **CORRUPT** - Rotten, degenerate

- **REVELATION** - Unveiling or making-known (applied to truths about God)

- **SCRIPTURE** - Bible - passages having authority

- **REGENERATION** - Making better/healthy

- **ACCOMMODATION** - Making room for

KNOWLEDGE OF GOD'S EXISTENCE

Reflection: What is true knowledge? Is it scientific, philosophical or religious? In other words, is there something called wisdom which somehow transcends factual or logical knowledge? Some have claimed that knowledge of God is the supreme knowledge, and that other knowledge is inferior.

In theology, the debate about what constitutes true knowledge has usually been studied under the heading of **NATURAL & REVEALED KNOWLEDGE**. Natural knowledge is any knowledge we can gain of God from the world, and revealed knowledge is God making Himself known to humans without means of the use of nature. Calvin considered that revealed knowledge was superior.

Natural Knowledge of God's Existence as an Innate Human Sense of the Divine

JOHN CALVIN has had an influential hand in the debate about how we can have knowledge of God. He claims that we can have a knowledge of God through various elements of creation, both in ourselves, and in nature and history.

Calvin posits two main grounds for knowledge of God: a subjective and an objective ground. The subjective ground has been termed above **AN INNATE HUMAN SENSE OF THE DIVINE**.

This is termed by Calvin the sensus divinitatis (sense of divinity) or semen religionis (seed of religion). It has been planted by God in every human. We all, by virtue of being created by God, have an inbuilt sense of our Creator. This could be called a disposition to believe in God. Calvin argues that this can be seen through:

- **THE UNIVERSALITY OF RELIGION** - This means that all humans respond to beauty and goodness and make attempts to build structures of meaning on these responses - this is religion. They are responding to God through the beauty and goodness they see.

- **THE TROUBLED CONSCIENCE** - All humans have a sense of guilt (or at least the majority do!), and this is because they are aware that they are responsible before God for their actions.

- **SERVILE FEAR OF GOD** - The desire to serve God in fear of His judgement upon them

These can all be seen as points of contact for the Christian revelation in the Gospel. However, Calvin does not believe these are proofs of innate knowledge of God - they do not lead to true knowledge of God. True knowledge of God can only come through a personal encounter with Him.

Natural Knowledge of God's Existence As Seen in the Order of Creation

The second, objective ground for knowledge of God is what can be seen in the apparent design and purpose of nature. My experience of the natural order, along with my contemplation of it, is a basis for knowledge of God.

CALVIN argues that the creation is a **MIRROR OF GOD**:

"This skilful ordering of the universe is for us a sort of mirror in which we can contemplate God, who is otherwise invisible".

Calvin, Institutes, I. V. 1

This is essentially a kind of design argument - the beauty and grandeur of the world can lead us to an appreciation of God its creator.

However, it is not meant as a proof of God's existence, for instance, as many see Aquinas' Fifth Way. Calvin intends it to be a demonstration of what we can learn about God's nature from creation.

Calvin makes a distinction between appearance and essence - he says the creation is the appearance of God's nature, which means that although we might be able to learn something of God's mercy or justice from the creation, it would be remote knowledge, and not true knowledge.

For instance, if I had only interacted with someone on social media and never met them in real life, I would only have a knowledge of them based on what they had decided to put online - which might be very remote from what they were really like (even though I would probably have a general idea of what they were like). In the case of a friend that I have known since school, however, I would have much truer knowledge of what they were like.

Revealed Knowledge of God's Existence Through Faith and God's Grace

It is theoretically possible for natural knowledge, knowledge as gained from reflection on creation and the sensus divinitatis, to lead humans to God. However, Calvin thought there was a major problem with this type of knowledge. It is not just that we can only gain an appearance of God from this type of knowledge, not just that our limited minds can only weakly know what God is like in this way. It is that, as Augustine emphasised, if the whole human being has been radically corrupted by the effects of **ORIGINAL SIN** contracted from the Fall, then that means our faculty of knowing God has also been **CORRUPTED**.

There is a great distance in knowledge between us and God, which is increased by our Fall. This means that natural knowledge of God is completely inadequate as a basis for a relationship with Him.

However, this is not the end of the story; God has, out of His love for humanity, stepped towards us and revealed himself to us in the person of **JESUS CHRIST**. This is what the Christian faith claims, and it is this second type of knowledge, revealed knowledge, that Calvin says is a fuller and more complete knowledge of God.

Calvin puts it like this:

> *"The knowledge of God, which is clearly shown in the ordering of the world and in all creatures, is still more clearly and familiarly explained in the Word."*

Calvin's argument could be summarised in this way. Revealed knowledge is superior because:

- **IT IS REVELATION** - As the revelation of the Word of God, it can lead humans to a fuller knowledge of His divine nature

- **SCRIPTURE** - Is essentially the revelation of the redemptive action of God in history, and particularly in the person of Christ, His life, death and resurrection

- **GOD THROUGH CHRIST** - We can only know God fully as mediated through Jesus Christ, and we can only know Christ fully through scripture

- **REGENERATION** - Knowledge of God in this way Calvin calls regeneration - to be renewed, restored and recreated through saving knowledge of Christ

- **ACCOMMODATION** - Christ reflects God's love, mercy and so on to us in a way that is appropriate for our Fallen condition - Calvin calls this accommodation - God accommodates Himself to us so that we may know Him

Therefore, Calvin argues that there is **DOUBLE GRACE** in Christ - grace of repentance given through Christ's death and resurrection, and grace of justification as humans are re-aligned with God.

Discussion points

Did Calvin, in emphasising the difference between God as Creator and God the Redeemer in Christ, actually create a dualistic theology, with two very different notions of God? Some argue that Calvin has a natural theology, whilst others argue that he limits himself to revealed theology, using the limitations of natural theology as a contrast.

In stressing the personal relationship with Christ, and thus placing emphasis on scripture as the means of access to this relationship, Calvin seems to dismiss the idea that faith or saving knowledge is possible through a corporate knowledge of Christ in the sacraments and through the life of the Church.

Can faith alone be a sufficient reason for belief in God? Many have come to believe in God through a process of intellectual exploration, by which they have become more and more convinced. Although for those people, rational argument may not have been the whole story, it has nonetheless been a foundational element of their faith journey.

It is possible that revealed knowledge of God is not really different to natural knowledge - is it possible to distinguish them? Calvin does claim there is not a sharp distinction, but that scripture does clarify and extend what can be known through nature.

NEED MORE HELP ON THE EXISTENCE OF GOD?

Use your phone to scan this QR code

Person of Jesus Christ

AUTHORITY is the key to this module. Consider what we mean when we say someone has authority. We may mean they have a kind of charisma, or we might mean that they have been given that authority by virtue of their position in an organisation, or because of who they are. For instance, as a mother or father, someone has the authority to discipline or reward their child.

KEYWORDS

- **AUTHORITY** - The influence that a person or thing has to command respect of others
- **SONSHIP** - Term used to describe relationship Christians have with God through baptism
- **MIRACLE** - Unexplained event with a supernatural origin
- **LIBERATION THEOLOGY** - Politically-based theology which emphasises Jesus' role as liberator of poor and oppressed
- **BLACK THEOLOGY** - Theology which emphasises Jesus' outsider status and ability to speak for racial minorities today
- **BLACK MESSIAH** - Idea of Jesus as being able to speak as authority for black people because of his Jewishness and minority status
- **OPPRESSION** - Unequal treatment of a group of people by a government
- **MARGINALISATION** - State of being made to feel an outsider and beyond the reach of society
- **LESSING'S DITCH** - Term for the distance between the non-rational 'mythical' elements of scripture and modern liberal beliefs

When we come to look at the way Jesus' authority is interpreted, we can see different viewpoints. Views on Jesus' authority take different forms:

JESUS CHRIST'S AUTHORITY AS THE SON OF GOD

Throughout the New Testament it is possible to see examples of the divinity of Jesus. One such way is expressed in his knowledge of God.

Knowledge of God

It can be clearly seen that Christ knows God in ways that others don't. Some examples of his knowledge of God include:

- **BELOVED SON** - At his baptism the voice of God says "this is my beloved Son".

- **ABBA** - He seems to have a personal relationship with him calling him "Abba", roughly translated as "dad".

- **DIVINE LIGHT** - Theologians have taught that "the soul of Christ from the beginning is elevated to participation in the divine wisdom by an infusion of Divine light." (Catholic Encyclopedia).

- **BEATIFIC VISION** - The basis for this beatific vision is the hypostatic union of Christ's human soul with the Word. In other words, because Christ was truly man and truly God, he was blessed with the immediate knowledge of God that is appropriate to that state. Another way of putting this is that as Christ is the Son of God, it would not be right of a good and loving father to deprive his son of the sight of his face.

There are many examples of Christ's immediate knowledge of the Father in scripture. For instance, Jesus says:

- **JOHN 3:11** - "Believe me, we speak of what is known to us, and testify of what our eyes have seen".

- **JOHN 1:18** - "No man has ever seen God; but now his only-begotten Son, who abides in the bosom of the Father, has himself become our interpreter".

- **ADOPTED SONSHIP** - Christ's knowledge of God as Son of God is seen to be foundational for Christians' knowledge of God (indeed, Christians often talk of an adopted **SONSHIP** - we are made God's sons by baptism - Christ of course was **GOD'S OWN SON**, and not adopted).

- **AUTHORITATIVE SONSHIP** - When Christ says "I am the Way and the Truth and the Life; no-one comes to the Father except through me", we can clearly understand how His Sonship is authoritative for Christians; essentially knowledge of Jesus through following on the Way with Him is the same as knowledge of God.

Miracles

Jesus' miracles are perhaps the clearest demonstration of his power and authority as the Son of God. The Gospel writers, particularly John, often underscore their importance with sayings of Jesus - these help to bring out the message of the miracle more fully and thus help believers to come to a fuller understanding of the person of Christ.

Some miracles in particular help us to get a sense of the authority of Christ as the Son of God:

- **MARK 6:47-52** - Christ walks on the water to the boat. Not only does this demonstrate the power of Christ over the water which should have swallowed him up, but it echoes the creative power of God who hovers over the waters (formless chaos) on the first day of creation, imprinting order on them. Again, it has echoes of Moses parting the Red Sea; the wind and the waves are making it hard going for the disciples, but Christ calms the wind and gets into the boat with them, taking them safely across.

- **REVELATION TO MOSES** - One particular feature of this miracle helps us to get a sense of the divinity of Christ - he says "It is I; do not be afraid", which would be better rendered as "I am; do not be afraid" (ego eimi or ego sum). "I am" is the name that God gives Himself in His revelation to Moses.

- **JOHN 9:1-41** - The miracle of the healing of the man born blind in St. John's Gospel. This is a highly complex passage containing many layers of meaning along the theme of light, darkness, sight and blindness. It illuminates the status of Jesus as the one sent into the world as revealer of Truth, which truth involves a moral movement on the part of humans to either be filled with one's own self, and thus to be in darkness, or to be empty of self and thus to be capable of being filled with the light of Christ.

- **BLIND HEALING** - The man born blind prostrates himself at the feet of Christ after his healing, and is thus able to see not only physically but spiritually - he comes to see that Christ is the Son of God; the Pharisees doubt the testimony of the man, and thus make themselves spiritually blind.

- **SELF-REVELATIONS** - We see that Jesus' miracles in John's Gospel are self-revelations of Christ as the Son of the Father.

The Resurrection

The central miracle, the central event, in the Gospels is the resurrection. Without it, Paul says, faith would be in vain, "because you would still be in your sins". This means that through his death and resurrection Jesus redeems humanity, and provides the basis for a relationship with God.

If the incarnation marks the **ENTRANCE** of the supernatural into the fallen world, then the resurrection is the exit door, but it is not an escape route, rather it is a '"Taking-up" of creation into the bosom of the father; it means that the world is not condemned to go the way of corruption, but that by cooperating with the will of the father the whole of creation can be redeemed.

The resurrection shows Jesus Christ's authority in the ultimate way, as Christus Victor, or Christ triumphant, who conquers over sin and death. It provides hope for Christians.

> ▶ **DISCUSSION** - *Did Jesus think of himself as divine?*
>
> ▪ **FOR** - There seems to be little evidence that this was the case. **N T WRIGHT** argues that it would have been highly unlikely that the disciples would have behaved in this fashion. There are many sayings of Jesus in which he seems to proclaim his divinity or unique status: "I am the Way, the Truth and the Life, He who eats my body and drinks my blood has eternal life" and so on.
>
> ▪ **AGAINST** - **SCHWEITZER** argues that Jesus thought of himself as a prophet announcing the end of the world. The quest for the historical Jesus had shown that actually he was a Jewish reformer who failed and was executed - in a kind of denial of this failure his followers had invented the resurrection and claimed his divinity.

JESUS CHRIST'S AUTHORITY AS A TEACHER OF WISDOM

Jesus is revered as a teacher throughout the New Testament. He is a **NEW MOSES**, who comes to fulfil the Law. In the Sermon on the Mount in chapters 5 to 7 of Matthew's Gospel there is an extended discourse by Jesus which contains the essence of His teaching. Some key aspects are:

▸ ## Jesus' moral teaching on repentance and forgiveness:

Jesus demands perfection, not in the sense of flawlessness, but in terms of always striving to do the will of the Father. For this reason, he says that before you worship God, you must make sure that you are in the right relation to those around you (Matt 5:23-26).

This sense of being on good terms goes beyond simply paying another what you owe them or asking their forgiveness; it involves an active love of others, not merely by not retaliating if they seek to harm you, but offering back love instead of hate. (Matt 5:38-48)

In this sense the saying of Jesus that "By the measure with which you measure will you be measured" illuminates what our actions to others should be. We cannot simply go by the old law of "an eye for an eye and a tooth for a tooth" - God requires more of us.

▸ ## Jesus' teaching on inner purity and moral motivation

In Matt 5:27-32 Jesus outlines his teaching on inner purity. It might at first sight seem radical, but it is really just bringing out the inner meaning of certain of the Commandments. He states that if your eye causes you to lust, you should pluck it out, for it's better to lose one part of yourself than that the whole of you should fall into hell.

This is using **RABBINIC HYPERBOLE** to make a point - there are occasions of sin which can be so damaging that it is best to remove yourself from them. If you look lustfully at someone, then in a sense in your heart you have already committed the act. If later you actually do commit adultery it will only be a consequence of the original lustful thought. Of course, many lustful thoughts remain as only thoughts, but it is rare that an act of adultery is not preceded by a series of lustful thoughts.

The connection between the commandment "do not commit adultery" and "do not covet your neighbour's wife" is here brought out - the latter is prior to the former (even though it comes after it in the Decalogue), and thus in a sense more serious. Without it you might not commit adultery

The importance of purity of heart is further brought out in the beatitudes: Jesus says:

"Blessed are the pure in heart, for they shall see God".

To be able to govern one's imagination is utterly necessary if one is to proceed on the spiritual path - this is the inner meaning of the vow of chastity which is taken by the religious.

It is more than mere prudery or observing propriety; governing one's response to others means not acting on the inclinations of the lower self. Elsewhere Jesus says "The eye is the lamp of the body, if your eye is single, your whole body will be full of light". Looking lustfully at another is a kind of grasping which has the effect of darkening what should be light.

This teaching on inner purity is part of Jesus' broader teaching that what makes us unclean is what comes from us, our thoughts and words, rather than what goes into us, eg. food.

▸ **DISCUSSION** - *Are Jesus' teachings coherent if separated from His divine status?*

■ **YES** - However, Lewis oversimplifies rather drastically as **N. T. WRIGHT** points out:

"What Lewis totally failed to see - as have, of course, many scholars in the field - was that Judaism already had a strong incarnational principle, namely the Temple, and that the language used of Shekinah, Torah, Wisdom, Word, and Spirit in the Old Testament - the language, in other words, upon which the earliest Christians drew when they were exploring and expounding what we have called Christology - was a language designed, long before Jesus'[s] day, to explain how the one true God could be both transcendent over the world and living and active within it, particularly within Israel. Lewis, at best, drastically short-circuits the argument. When Jesus says, 'Your sins are forgiven,' he is not claiming straightforwardly to be God, but to give people, out on the street, what they would normally get by going to the Temple."

(Touchstone magazine, March 2007)

■ **NO** - As C S Lewis said:

"I am trying here to prevent anyone saying the really foolish thing that people often say about Him: I'm ready to accept Jesus as a great moral teacher, but I don't accept his claim to be God. That is the one thing we must not say. A man who was merely a man and said the sort of things Jesus said would not be a great moral teacher. He would either be a lunatic - on the level with the man who says he is a poached egg - or else he would be the Devil of Hell. You must make your choice. Either this man was, and is, the Son of God, or else a madman or something worse. You can shut him up for a fool, you can spit at him and kill him as a demon or you can fall at his feet and call him Lord and God, but let us not come with any patronizing nonsense about his being a great human teacher. He has not left that open to us. He did not intend to."

JESUS CHRIST'S AUTHORITY AS A LIBERATOR OF THE MARGINALISED AND THE POOR

At several points in the New Testament Jesus clearly challenges political and religious authority. Some modern theologians have emphasised this aspect of his mission in order to create **LIBERATION THEOLOGIES** which show the concern with the poor and marginalised in society.

One example of a theologian who has emphasised Jesus' role as subversive of the status quo and champion of the oppressed is James Cone. He founded **BLACK THEOLOGY**; in his book God of the Oppressed he says:

> *"Jesus Christ is the subject of Black Theology because he is the content of the hopes and dreams of black people."*

Cone argues that the term **BLACK MESSIAH** is an appropriate one for Jesus. Cone says "He is black because he was a Jew". He argues that theology needs to be contextualised - too often white theologians have ignored the ethnic background of Jesus in an attempt to universalise him.

As Moses led his people out of slavery, Jesus is the leader of a new exodus, someone who can liberate his people from **OPPRESSION** and **MARGINALISATION**.

Some Bible passages bring out this aspect of Jesus' ministry:

▸ ## The woman with the haemorrhage (Mark 5:24-34)

The radical nature of what Jesus does in this miracle is perhaps easy to miss in modern times, but it is hard to think of a more marginalised person than this woman. The rules about ritual uncleanliness meant that this woman with heavy bleeding would have been ostracised from normal Jewish life for 12 years. What she does, merely touching the hem of Jesus' cloak, transgresses the rules. Jesus does not respond with anger, but merely tells the woman that her faith has healed her.

Culturally and in religious terms, this woman's illness has made her into someone who has lost her life. Her faith in Jesus restores that life.

▸ ## The parable of the Good Samaritan (Luke 10: 25-37)

Who is my neighbour? Jesus responds with a parable which challenges normal answers to that question. Your neighbour is anyone in need. And again, religious and cultural rules matter less than loving actions to the person in front of you who is in need.

▶ **DISCUSSION** - *Was Jesus more than just a political liberator?*

■ **LIBERATION THEOLOGY** - Clearly Jesus's message can be interpreted politically - Liberation Theology is a clear example of that, but many would argue that his message of redemption cannot be reduced to the merely political, even though it might have profound political effects if lived out in the community

■ **LESSING'S DITCH** - There are some liberal theologians who might want to argue that what is non-rational in Jesus' message (eg. miracles, divinity sayings etc.) should be jettisoned; in that case what remains might be overtly a message of political liberation come again to judge mankind, that he and the father were one, precluded him from being simply a moral teacher.

NEED MORE HELP ON THE PERSON OF JESUS CHRIST?

Use your phone to scan this QR code

Martin Luther

Christian Moral Principles

Christian ethics has traditionally been seen to derive its authority from three main sources - Bible, Church and reason. Here we will examine challenges to this view, and explore the role of scripture in ethical decision-making, especially as regards the authority it has in relation to what is called Sacred Tradition.

KEYWORDS

- **BIBLICIST** - Believer in absolute literal truth of Bible texts

- **FUNDAMENTALIST** - 19th century American Protestant reaction to theological modernism, placing emphasis on truth of scripture over interpretations which accommodated evolution etc.

- **DIVINE DICTATION** - Belief that God has dictated the truths of the Bible to scribes word for word

- **INERRANT** - Incapable of error

- **DECALOGUE** - Ten commandments

- **PARADIGM** - Model or blueprint

- **WORD OF GOD** - Belief that Bible is inspired and contains truth made known by God

- **LITERALIST** - See Biblicist

- **CCC** - Catechism of the Catholic Church

- **DEPOSIT OF THE FAITH** - Traditions and belief passed on by believers; collection of what has always been believed by the faithful

- **MAGISTERIUM** - Teaching authority of the Church

- **TRIANGULATION** - Process of orientating one's self in space

- **CONSCIENCE** - Faculty of knowing what is right and acting in accordance with it

THE DIVERSITY OF CHRISTIAN MORAL REASONING AND PRACTICES AND SOURCES OF ETHICS

There are three main views on the sources of authority for Christian moral principles. Firstly, those who believe that the Bible is the sole authority for Christian ethical practices, secondly the view that the Bible, Church and reason together are sources of authority, and thirdly, that love is the only source of authority for moral principles, and that reason must decide how to apply it.

Bible as the Sole Authority

This view would be favoured by the **BIBLICISTS** or **FUNDAMENTALISTS** - those who view the Bible as the exact words of God. This is sometimes called **DIVINE DICTATION**, the view that the writers of the Bible were just dictated to by God and wrote down what He said. Clearly if the Bible is viewed in this way, then it will be supremely authoritative for Christian ethics.

In this view the Bible **CANNOT ERR** (is **INERRANT**) when it comes to judgements relating to matters of ethics or moral behaviour and there is often an assumption that any moral content of the Bible will be in the form of a **SET OF RULES**. The **DECALOGUE** (Exodus 20: 1-17) is a clear example of this.

In many Old Testament books there are very specific rules regarding all aspects of life:

- **MORAL CONTENT** - Viewing the moral content of the Bible as simply a set of rules profoundly misunderstands it - even the Decalogue comes as part of the story of God's covenant with Israel.

- **SYMBOLIC FORM** - Much moral content of the Bible comes in story or narrative or symbolic form - Richard Hays says that in the New Testament we are likely to encounter ethical content in one of three ways - through principles, paradigms or a symbolic world.

- **GUIDELINES** - Principles are general guidelines (eg. love God and your neighbour) of which you must then work out the specifics of how to apply.

- **PARADIGMS** - These are stories with examples of behaviour to either follow or avoid. For instance, the story of the widow's mite (Mark 12: 41-44).

- **SYMBOLIC WORLD** - A symbolic world is a general picture of the world which includes the divine element. We have to work out how to orient ourselves within this world. In this picture God might appear as a kind of role model whom we can look to. For instance, in the **SERMON ON THE MOUNT** Jesus says that we should aim to be perfect as our Father in heaven is perfect.

Bible, Church and Reason as the Sources of Christian Ethical Practices

For the reasons just mentioned, if the moral content of the Bible is not straightforwardly a set of rules but rather a less specific ethical narrative, then it makes much more sense in moral decision-making to have sources of authority outside of the Bible which can be used in combination with it.

This is the position of the Roman **CATHOLIC CHURCH**. It views the Bible as the **WORD OF GOD**, and therefore inerrant, but not as "divine dictation" - the Bible was inspired by God, but nonetheless it is a collection of writings from different times, people and cultures, and needs interpreting. Equally, as the Bible contains many different kinds of writing such as poetry, parables and history, there cannot be one simple **LITERALIST** interpretation of everything in it.

The **CCC** (Catechism of the Catholic Church) says:

> *"Sacred Tradition and Sacred Scripture are bound closely together and communicate one with the other. For both of them, flowing out of the divine well-spring come together in some fashion to form one thing, and move towards the same goal"*

What is Sacred Tradition?

The CCC says:

> *"In order that the full and living Gospel might always be preserved in the Church the apostles left Bishops as their successors … the apostolic preaching, which is expressed in a special way in the inspired books, was to be preserved in a continuous line of succession until the end of time … This living transmission, accomplished in the Holy Spirit, is called Tradition, since it is distinct from Sacred Scripture, though closely connected to it."*

There are therefore two distinct modes of transmission of the mystery of Christ, and -

> *"As a result the Church, to whom the transmission and interpretation of Revelation is entrusted, does not derive her certainty about all revealed truths from the holy scriptures alone. Both Scripture and Tradition must be accepted and honoured with equal sentiments of devotion and reverence."*

CCC 77-82

Indeed, there are also philosophical reasons why the Church does not rely solely on scripture for its certainty of moral truths. Chief of these is that if the Bible was to provide its own justification for belief in its truths then you have a classic example of circular reasoning, which is fallacious.

For example, circular reasoning in conversation might look like this:

- **The Bible is the Word of God**

- How can you be so sure?

- **Because the Bible tells us so**

- But why believe the Bible?

- **Because the Bible is infallible**

- But how do you know it is infallible?

- **Because the Bible is the Word of God**

- And so on ...

So alongside Scripture, many Christians also place the living tradition of the Church. Together these two are known in the Catholic tradition as the **DEPOSITUM FIDEI**, or **DEPOSIT OF THE FAITH**.

There is a third element, which is that of reason. Reason is exercised through the **MAGISTERIUM** of the Church, which is the teaching authority of the Church. Reason is also exercised through the individual conscience of the lay person .

These three elements, one's own reasoning combined with that of the Church, the Tradition of the Church and Holy Scripture, should all be consulted when forming a moral position, according to Catholics.

One clear advantage of this is that it allows a kind of moral **TRIANGULATION** to take place (essentially, you can compare your own decision with two other sources of authority, which enables you to be surer of the direction you should take).

However, if one's own **CONSCIENCE** is in radical disagreement with scripture, or Church tradition seems to go against what you believe and scripture seems to say, then it would seem a terrible muddle, and not at all clear as to how to make a decision.

Is Love the only Christian Ethical Principle Which Governs Christian Practices?

"I may speak with every tongue that men and angels use; yet, if I lack charity, I am no better than echoing bronze, or the clash of cymbals. I may have powers of prophecy, no secret hidden from me, no knowledge too deep for me; I may have utter faith, so that I can move mountains; yet if I lack charity, I count for nothing. I may give away all that I have, to feed the poor; I may give myself up to be burnt at the stake; if I lack charity, it goes for nothing. Charity is patient, is kind; charity feels no envy; charity is never perverse or proud, never insolent; does not claim its rights, cannot be provoked, does not brood over an injury; takes no pleasure in wrong-doing, but rejoices at the victory of truth; sustains, believes, hopes, endures, to the last."

1 Corinthians 13: 1-7

The above passage gives weight to this third view that love or agape is the only Christian ethical principle.

Much work on this view was done in the twentieth century by Joseph Fletcher, who formulated what he called Situation Ethics to describe the process of moral decision-making in which only love is the supreme principle, and we must use our reason to decide how to apply this principle in different situations. For more information, see the Religion and Ethics section of this Guide.

▶ **DISCUSSION** - *Are Christian ethics personal or communal?*

■ **GILBERT MEILAENDER** - A Christian bioethicist - said: "What makes us true individuals … is that God calls us by name. Our individuality is not a personal achievement or power, and - most striking of all - it is established only in community with God. We are most ourselves not when we seek to direct and control our destiny but when we recognize and admit that our life is grounded in and sustained by God."

■ **THE OUR** in the **OUR FATHER PRAYER** - Is an indicator of the communal nature of Christian ethics - Christians leave their individualism behind because in building up the Kingdom of God on earth there can be no divisions or conflict, and in prayer they pray as one body - the Church is the Body of Christ.

■ **INDIVISIBILITY** - True Christian Ethics recognises this indivisibility of all people in Christ, and understands that no moral decision is made in isolation from the community of others in which one finds one's self.

▶ **DISCUSSION** - *Is the Bible a comprehensive moral guide?*

■ **TOM DEIDUN** - Doubts that it is. He points out that the diversity of material in the Bible, coupled with the contextual and cultural differences between the modern age and that of the Bible, means that it is very difficult, perhaps impossible, to find a coherent overall ethical message in it.

■ **RICHARD HAYS** - Is more optimistic. He argues that New Testament ethics has a 'fourfold task' which includes sorting through the problems just discussed in the following stages: descriptive, synthetic, hermeneutical and pragmatic. In the synthetic stage Hays argues that we should see if any coherent general message arises from the different texts.

■ **SOLE SOURCE** - However, neither of these scholars would argue that the Bible alone can be the sole source of authority for morality - even Hays is applying reason and teaching to the scripture passages.

NEED MORE HELP ON CHRISTIAN MORAL PRINCIPLES?

Use your phone to scan this QR code

Dietrich Bonhoeffer

Christian Moral Action

When we come to examine Christian morality, we might observe that without a proper understanding of Christ's words regarding discipleship, suffering and the cross, and the central place of Christ's own crucifixion in the Gospels, Christians risk moral action becoming a form of self-expression, rather than a radical submission to the will of God, and a consequent ability to put one's self at the service of those in need.

KEYWORDS

- **CHRISTIAN ETHICS** - Any system of ethics with a Christian basis, such as natural law

- **DISCIPLESHIP** - The state of following Jesus Christ

- **CHEAP GRACE** - Bonhoeffer's phrase for the belief that we are saved without any moral effort on our part

- **COSTLY GRACE** - Bonhoeffer's phrase for the Gospel requirement of repentance and conversion of life to be saved

- **PROSPERITY GOSPEL** - Charismatic Christian belief that God rewards faith with financial reward

- **SACRIFICE** - The act of giving up an attachment to something you hold dear

- **KENOSIS** - From the Greek, meaning "emptying-out", used to describe Christ's giving of his life for others

THE TEACHING AND EXAMPLE OF DIETRICH BONHOEFFER

DIETRICH BONHOEFFER (1906-45) was a theologian living and working in Germany at the time of the rise to power of Hitler. His distinctive contribution to modern theology was not just in his teaching but in the example he set. His analysis of the cultural situation within which Christ's message is proclaimed is profound.

But he also lived the message that he taught. On April 5, 1943, Bonhoeffer was arrested for his involvement in a plot to assassinate Adolf Hitler. He spent 18 months in Berlin's Tegel prison, and was shot shortly before the end of the war.

Before the war he had gone to America and had planned to live there, but decided that he needed to be with his fellow Christians in Germany, even though he knew that this put him in danger.

Bonhoeffer argued for a **RELIGIONLESS CHRISTIANITY**, which is not a call to disband any formal churches, but rather a critique of theologies which argued that man was naturally religious. He could not accept that at a time when such a powerfully secular world was coming to birth.

Bonhoeffer on Duty to God and the State

Bonhoeffer grounds his interpretation of ethics in Christ himself. He says:

> *"The subject matter of a Christian ethic is God's reality revealed in Christ becoming real among God's creatures, just as the subject matter of doctrinal theology is the truth of God's reality revealed in Christ."*

Dietrich Bonhoeffer, "Christ, Reality, and Good. Christ Church, and World,"

As Christ is Lord of all, a truly Christian ethics will have its source in Christ and lead to Christ. Because Christ is Lord of all Creation He cannot be "a partial reality alongside others." Bonhoeffer writes;

> *"The world belongs to Christ, and only in Christ is the world what it is. It needs, therefore, nothing less than Christ himself. Everything would be spoiled if we were to reserve Christ for the church while granting the world only some law, Christian though it may be. Christ has died for the world, and Christ is Christ only in the midst of the world."*

In April 1933 Bonhoeffer laid out three ways the Church can act towards the state:

- **BE RESPONSIBLE** - The church can "ask the state whether its actions are legitimate and in accordance with its character as state, i.e. it can throw the state back on its responsibilities."

- **AID THE VICTIMS** - The church must "aid the victims of state action. The church has an unconditional obligation to the victims of any ordering of society, even if they do not belong to the Christian community." These first two ways are common for the church according to Bonhoeffer, as government is necessarily flawed and results in injustices which vary in type, but are always there.

- **PUT A SPOKE IN THE WHEEL** - The third way of action for the church is rarer and more serious as it means "not just to bandage the victims under the wheel, but to put a spoke in the wheel itself. Such action would be direct political action, and is only possible and desirable when the church sees the state fail in its function of creating law and order." Bonhoeffer believed that this type of action is only possible when the State is in the process of 'negating itself' by ordering things which go against the common good.

Bonhoeffer on the cost of discipleship

Bonhoeffer's teaching on ethics as action are based on his understanding of God. Bonhoeffer works on the assumption that our understanding of Christ essentially forms our understanding of God. As Alister McGrath puts it he "interprets the powerlessness of the crucified Christ as a paradigm for the powerlessness of God in the world."

In his Letters and Papers from Prison, Bonhoeffer spells out what this means for Christian ethics:

> *"The God who is with us is the God who forsakes us (Mark 15:34). The God who lets us live in the world without the working hypothesis of God is the God before whom we stand continually. Before God and with God we live without God. God lets himself be pushed out of the world on to the cross. He is weak and powerless in the world, and that is precisely the way, the only way, in which he is with us and helps us. Matt. 8:17 makes it quite clear that Christ helps us, not by virtue of his omnipotence, but by virtue of his weakness and suffering."*

We can see from this that Bonhoeffer identifies in the profound suffering of Christ, the very way that God is with us. Equally, it is through this suffering and weakness that we can be followers of Christ. He makes this even clearer elsewhere:

> *"***CHEAP GRACE*** - Means grace sold on the market like cheapjacks' wares. The sacraments, the forgiveness of sin, and the consolations of religion are thrown away at cut prices. Grace is represented as the Church's inexhaustible treasury, from which she showers blessings with generous hands, without asking questions or fixing limits. Grace without price; grace without cost! The essence of grace, we suppose, is that the account has been paid in advance; and, because it has been paid, everything can be had for nothing. Since the cost was infinite, the possibilities of using and spending it are infinite. What would grace be if it were not cheap?... "*

> *"Cheap grace is the preaching of forgiveness without requiring repentance, baptism without church discipline, Communion without confession, absolution without personal confession. Cheap grace is grace without discipleship, grace without the cross, grace without Jesus Christ, living and incarnate."*

> *"***COSTLY GRACE*** - The treasure hidden in the field; for the sake of it a man will go*

and sell all that he has. It is the pearl of great price to buy which the merchant will sell all his goods. It is the kingly rule of Christ, for whose sake a man will pluck out the eye which causes him to stumble; it is the call of Jesus Christ at which the disciple leaves his nets and follows him.

Costly grace is the gospel which must be sought again and again, the gift which must be asked for, the door at which a man must knock.

Such grace is costly because it calls us to follow, and it is grace because it calls us to follow Jesus Christ. It is costly because it costs a man his life, and it is grace because it gives a man the only true life. It is costly because it condemns sin, and grace because it justifies the sinner. Above all, it is costly because it cost God the life of his Son: "ye were bought at a price," and what has cost God much cannot be cheap for us. Above all, it is grace because God did not reckon his Son too dear a price to pay for our life, but delivered him up for us. Costly grace is the Incarnation of God."

Much has been written about this idea of cheap and costly grace. Bonhoeffer touches on some profound points which we can trace all the way back to Augustine.

The doctrine of election that Calvin developed has had the effect of creating strands of Christianity in which the only question is whether you have accepted Christ. Nothing further is required, no striving, no humility, poverty of spirit, taking up your cross, leaving behind all worldly goods; all these essentials of Christian discipleship are forgotten about or ignored.

For instance, what is called the **PROSPERITY GOSPEL** would be one example of this at work. Part of many types of Charismatic movements, the Prosperity Gospel claims that God rewards faith with financial reward.

Clearly aberrations, such movements have come to prominence in recent times, and Bonhoeffer's words have come to seem prophetic - what he saw happening in the Church in the 1930s is even more evident now.

SACRIFICE AND SUFFERING

Bonhoeffer's teachings and life are supreme examples of the idea of Christian discipleship as involving sacrifice and suffering. Here are some Gospel passages which illustrate the importance of this:

- **MARK 8:34-37** - Then he called the crowd to him along with his disciples and said:"Whoever wants to be my disciple must deny themselves and take up their cross and follow me. For whoever wants to save their life will lose it, but whoever loses their life for me and for the gospel will save it. What good is it for someone to gain the whole world, yet forfeit their soul? Or what can anyone give in exchange for their soul?

- **JOHN 12:24** - Truly, truly I say to you; unless a grain of wheat falls into the earth and dies, it remains alone; but if it dies, it bears much fruit. The one who loves his life will lose it, and the one who hates his life in this world will keep it for eternal life. If anyone serves Me, he must follow Me. Where I am, there My servant also will be. If anyone serves Me, the Father will honor him.

- **MATTHEW 7:13** - Enter through the narrow gate. For wide is the gate and broad is the road that leads to destruction, and many enter through it. But small is the gate and narrow the road that leads to life, and only a few find it.

These passages are very clear on discipleship - it involves taking a hard path; a path of **KENOSIS**, or self-emptying, pouring one's self out for others, dying to one's own lower desires and selfish inclinations. That is not going to be easy for anyone, but it is the pathway Christ asks people to follow.

This model of discipleship however, would make no sense if it were not the way to a profound happiness, deeper and greater than anything the world can give. Pope Benedict XVI puts it this way:

"Are we not perhaps all afraid in some way? If we let Christ enter fully into our lives, if we open ourselves totally to him, are we not afraid that He might take something away from us? Are we not perhaps afraid to give up something significant, something unique, something that makes life so beautiful? Do we not then risk ending up diminished and deprived of our freedom? And once again the Pope said: No! If we let Christ into our lives, we lose nothing, nothing, absolutely nothing of what makes life free, beautiful and great. No! Only in this friendship are the doors of life opened wide. Only in this friendship is the great potential of human existence truly revealed. Only in this friendship do we experience beauty and liberation. And so, today, with great strength and great conviction, on the basis of long personal experience of life, I say to

you, dear young people: Do not be afraid of Christ! He takes nothing away, and he gives you everything. When we give ourselves to him, we receive a hundredfold in return. Yes, open, open wide the doors to Christ – and you will find true life".

In this sense then, it must be that the sacrifice that discipleship involves means only a loss of what was never essential anyway:

"Store up treasure for yourselves in heaven, where moths and vermin do not destroy, and where robbers do not break in and steal"

Matt 6:20

> ▸ **DISCUSSION** - *Should Christians practise civil disobedience?*
>
> ■ **YES** - Lutheran Pastor Martin Luther King achieved great gains through his approach of non-violent civil disobedience, and this could be seen as completely in harmony with Gospel values.
>
> ■ **NO** - St Paul said Christians should obey the authorities, as they have been instituted by God.
>
> ■ **NON-INTERFERENCE** - Christ said "render unto Caesar what belongs to Caesar, and to God what belongs to God". This has been interpreted as "as long as the government does not interfere in the religious affairs of people, they should live according to its laws".

▶ **DISCUSSION** - *Does Bonhoeffer put too much emphasis on suffering?*

- **YES** - In light of Gospel passages such as: "I have come that they may have life to the full" some argue that Jesus' message was one of love, mercy and forgiveness, and that he came to bring us those gifts of healing by conferring on us the Holy Spirit. In this interpretation favoured by some Charismatic Christian groups, Jesus primarily came to preach the Good News, and was not sent by God to die on the cross, which they argue would be a monstrous act.

- **NO** - Of course, this ignores that God did not send his only Son simply to die, but to die and rise again, thus redeeming humanity. This central saving act of Christ- incarnation, death, resurrection and ascension- was one in which we must participate in some small way in our lives; Christians would point to baptism as the most obvious way in which this happens - we die to our old selves that we may be born anew. This is not a once-only event, but must be a daily event in the lives of Christians, who should follow in Christ's steps and serve others.

NEED MORE HELP ON CHRISTIAN MORAL ACTION?

Use your phone to scan this QR code

Lightning Source UK Ltd.
Milton Keynes UK
UKOW07f0854210917
309610UK00006B/335/P